Pass

The

Cabin Crew

Interview

In **24**

Hours

Pass

The
Cabin Crew
Interview

In **24**
Hours

First Edition
By Carrie Loren

Published by:

SpineBound
Bound to be Books

Pass the Cabin Crew Interview In **24** Hours
Simple Strategies for Quick Results

By Carrie Loren

© 2012 SpineBound Books and Carrie Loren

The right of Carrie Loren to be identified as the author of this work has been asserted in accordance with the Copyright, Design and Patents Act 1988

First Edition, 2012

ISBN 13:   9781908300034

Publisher's Note
Every possible effort has been made to ensure that the information contained in this book is accurate at the time of going to press, and the publishers and authors cannot accept responsibility for any errors or omissions, however caused. No responsibility for loss or damage occasioned to any person acting or refraining from action, as a result of the material in this publication can be accepted by the editor , the publisher or any of the authors.

British Library Cataloguing-in-Publication Data
A CIP catalogue record for this book can be obtained from the British library

Printed in the United Kingdom
10 9 8 7 6 5 4 3 2 1

Published by:

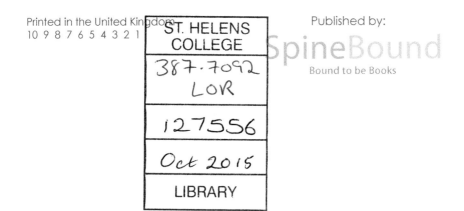

SpineBound
Bound to be Books

"Just as Carrie Loren urges those who read her book to do their research in seeking a cabin crew position, it is apparent that she has done hers in creating and writing this thorough and thoroughly engaging book."

Joseph Yurt - Reader Views

"If you are an applicant for cabin crew, Ms. Loren presents a thorough and well articulated set of tools for you. This book is a powerful guide for a far more comprehensive set of job seekers, and I give it a very strong endorsement."

William E. Cooper - Reader Views

"Dreaming of a career in the skies? Then Carrie Loren's new guide to getting hired by the airlines is what you need, A must-have for anyone wanting to be cabin crew."

Janet White - Author of Secrets of the Hidden Job Market

"If you want to get an idea of the cabin crew interview system then buy this. I am 42 yrs old, never had a flying job before, hadnt had an interview for a job in over 10 years. I needed to know what kind of things I would be asked and what to expect. I went for 3 cabin crew jobs and got all 3 of them offered to me. Need I say more???"

Rebecca Tapsell

"I contacted you when I was starting out my Cabin Crew Career and at the time you gave me lots of really good advice. Since securing my first Cabin Crew Job last year with Excel Airways I've been having a fantastic time working for a Swedish Airline, Viking. I even qualified as Senior Cabin Crew earlier in the year."

Camilla Gavin

"First of all, i'd like to say thank you for the precious book and all the important information you gave every time I wrote you. I'm so happy because they called from Emirates telling I was approved to work with them. I'm going to Dubai in January. I'd like to wish you a Merry Christmas and New Year full of happiness. Thank you once more i'll be in touch. A big Hug."

Claudia Mello

"The book is really amazing especially those question and answer part. Most of the answers really fits onto me while some of them serves as a correction from what i've done wrong. Its helps me in my present career as well as my personal developments. Most of them are exactly the words that describes me. I really like the content of the book. I felt like somebody intervied me and turn it to a manual. More power and God Bless!"

Redentor Tuazon

Contents

On Your Marks...

Prepare

Get Set...

Apply

Go...

Attend

Preface

On a beautiful late spring afternoon, two young women graduated from the same college. They were very much alike: both had been better than average students, both were personable and both shared a deep desire to travel the world and enter the highly competitive and coveted profession of Airline Cabin Crew.

Recently, these women returned to college for their tenth annual reunion. They were still very much alike and both, as it turned out, had gone to work for the same Airline after graduation. But, there was a difference.

One of the women was a customer support manager, while the other was part of the elite, world travelling cabin crew team.

What Made The Difference?

Have you ever wondered, what makes this kind of difference in people's lives? It isn't a native intelligence, nor talent or dedication. It isn't that one person wants success and the other doesn't. The difference lies in what each person knows and how he or she makes use of that knowledge.

That is the whole purpose of the book: to give you knowledge — knowledge that you can use to navigate the challenging road that 90% of applicants stumble and fail on. Now you can fast-track your way, with ease, to a glamorous career with your chosen airline, that will take you to exotic countries and hotels all around the world.

Within the pages of this book, you will be given a clear and effective blueprint to follow that will take you from scratch through to hearing 'you're hired' in the shortest time possible.

You will discover essential strategies and steps that you must know in order to be successful in one of the most competitive and sought after careers in the world.

Disclaimer

This book is designed to provide information and guidance on attending a cabin crew assessment. It is sold with the understanding that the publisher and author are not engaged in rendering legal or other professional services. Such topics, as discussed herein are, for example, or illustrative purposes only. If expert assistance is required, the services of a competent professional should be sought where you can explore the unique aspects of your situation and can receive specific advice tailored to your circumstances.

It is not the purpose of this guide to reprint all the information that is otherwise available to candidates but instead to complement, amplify and supplement other texts. You are urged to read all the available material, learn as much as possible about the role and interview techniques and tailor the information to your individual needs.

Every effort has been made to make this guide as complete and accurate as possible. However, this guide contains information that is current only up to the printing date. Interview processes are frequently updated and are often subject to differing interpretations. Therefore, there are no absolutes and this text should be used only as a general guide and not as the ultimate source of information.

All information in this book is offered as an opinion of the author and should be taken as such and used with discretion by the reader. You are solely responsible for your use of this book. Neither the publisher nor the author explicitly or implicitly promises that readers will find employment because of anything written or implied here.

The purpose of this guide is to educate and inform. The author and SpineBoudn Books shall have neither liability nor responsibility to you or anyone else because of any information contained in or left out of this book.

About Carrie Loren

Although I am now an interview coach, I too began my career as aspiring cabin crew.

From the age of 19, I spent several years going to interview after interview in pursuit of my dream. Unfortunately, I was clueless about the interview process and naive about the competition. With every rejection I experienced, my self esteem paid the price.

But I was determined to live my dream and never gave up.

Finally, after much research and preparation, I refined the process, perfected my technique and honed it down to a science. Then my pursuits began to pay off as I was hired by the largest airline in the Middle East, Emirates.

Since retiring from the skies, I have turned my passion to helping others achieve the same success and, over the past six years, I have used those same techniques to coach hundreds of candidates to interview success. Now, in this book, I will teach you those same techniques so you too can live your dream.

You already have the ability to get the job, you simply need to learn how.

Reach for the skies...

Part 1

Prepare

"It is not the will to win that matters, it is the
preparation to win that matters"

- Paul Bryant

01:00

Research the Airline

"An investment in knowledge pays the best interest"

- Benjamin Franklin

Preliminary Research

Taking the time to research the airline you want to work for will enable you to ask intelligent questions, as well as answer any that are posed.

Your informed knowledge will give a positive impression about you and your motivation to work for the airline, and give you a competitive edge over less informed candidates.

There is no need to know he whole history of the airline, but you should at least know some basic information, such as:

» What is their route network?

» Are there any future plans for expansion or growth?

» Where is their base airport located?

» Who are the airline's major competitors?

» What do you like about this particular airline?

» How long have they been operating?

» Has the airline won any awards? If so, which ones?

The airlines' literature and corporate website are great sources of this information. Don't forget to check the media or press section of the site for expansion news.

Selected Airline Facts

As noted on Wikipedia and correct at time of print

 Emirates Airline (EK)

Website:	www.emirates.com
Slogan:	Fly Emirates, Hello Tomorrow
Founded:	1985
Base:	Dubai International Airport, UAE
Frequent Flier Porgram:	Skywards
Fleet Size:	183 (As of September 2012)
Destinations:	125 (As of July 2012)
Key People:	Tim Clark (President)
	Ahmed Bin Saeed Al Maktoum (Chairman/CEO)

virgin atlantic Virgin Atlantic (VS)

Website:	www.virgin-atlantic.com
Founded:	1984
Base:	Gatwick & Heathrow Airport, UK
Frequent Flier Porgram:	Flying Club
Fleet Size:	41
Destinations:	35
Key People:	Sir Richard Branson (President)
	Stephen Murphy (Chairman)
	Steve Ridgway (CEO)

BRITISH AIRWAYS British Airways (BA)

Website:	www.britishairways.com
Slogan:	To Fly. To Serve
Founded:	1974
Base:	Heathrow Airport, UK
Frequent Flier Porgram:	Executive Club
Fleet Size:	241
Destinations:	169
Key People:	Keith Williams (CEO)
	Sir Martin Broughton (Chairman)

Southwest Airlines (WN)

Website: www.southwest.com
Slogan: Bags Fly Free
Founded: 1967
Base: T   exas, USA
Frequent Flier Porgram: Rapid Rewards
Fleet Size: 571
Destinations: 76
Key People: Herb Kelleher (Co-founder)
                            Rollin King (Co-founder)
                            Gary C. Kelly (Chairman, President, CEO)

Qantas (QF)

Website: www.qantas.com.au
Slogan: Spirit of Australia
Founded: 1920
Base: Sydney & Melbourne Airport, AU
Frequent Flier Porgram: Qantas Frequent Flier
Fleet Size: 145
Destinations: 41
Key People: Leigh Clifford, AO (Chairman)
                            Alan Joyce (CEO)

▲ DELTA Delta Airlines (DL)

Website: www.delta.com
Slogan: Keep Climbing
Founded: 1924
Base: Atlanta, Georgia. USA
Frequent Flier Porgram: Sky Miles
Fleet Size: 722
Destinations: 247
Key People: Richard H. Anderson (CEO)
                            Edward Bastian (President)

United Airlines (LA)

Website:	www.united.com
Slogan:	Keep Climbing
Founded:	1926
Frequent Flier Porgram:	Mileage Plus
Fleet Size:	705
Destinations:	378
Key People:	Jeffrey A. Smisek (CEO)
	Walter T. Varney (Founder)
	Glenn F. Tilton (Chairman)

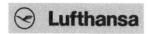

Lufthansa Airlines (LH)

Website:	www.lufthansa.com
Slogan:	Nonstop You
Founded:	1954
Base:	Frankfurt Airport, Germany
Frequent Flier Porgram:	Miles & More
Fleet Size:	279
Destinations:	221
Key People:	Jürgen Weber (Head of Supervisory Board)
	Christoph Franz (CEO)

AIRFRANCE Air France (AF)

Website:	www.airfrance.com
Slogan:	Making the sky the best place on Earth
Founded:	1933
Base:	Paris-Charles de Gaulle Airport, France
Frequent Flier Porgram:	Flying Blue
Fleet Size:	253
Destinations:	272
Key People:	Alexandre de Juniac (Chairman and CEO)

02:00

Prepare Yourself

> "You can't depend on your eyes when your imagination is out of focus"
>
> **- Mark Twain**

Our performance is dictated by our psychology. If our minds are preoccupied with doubt, we certainly won't perform well and are unlikely to be successful through each stage of the selection process.

Successful candidates share similar attitudes and beliefs, and have learned to manage their state. The good news is that these success patterns can be learned and duplicated. The following pages contain tips and techniques that will enable you to program your mind for success.

Manage your Mind Set

Limiting beliefs are erroneous assumptions we hold about our own capabilities. They lurk in our subconscious mind and lead to self-sabotaging behaviours which prevent us from achieving our desired goals. These beliefs are mostly acquired subconsciously through outside influences and, once accepted and imprinted into our subconscious mind, will dictate how well we perform, interact and grow.

To move forward, these limiting beliefs must be identified and challenged, and then replaced with empowering beliefs.

Identify
Clearly it would be impossible to challenge or change a belief that we are unaware of, so the first step to transformation involves identification.

Some limiting beliefs are obvious and can be easily identified by their all or nothing words, such as 'always' or 'never', or 'can't' or 'impossible'. For instance:

» My confidence always lets me down

» There's too much competition, I can't compete

» The interviews are impossible

» I never say the right thing

» I always fail

Some beliefs, however, are so deeply ingrained within our subconscious that we may not even be aware of their existence. To expose these, we can use a brainstorming session.

Brainstorming is a simple, yet powerful technique that produces raw material from the subconscious mind. To begin, simply sit down with a pad and pen and start writing down everything that comes to mind about the interview.

If you struggle for a place to begin, you could use the opening line "I want to pass the cabin crew interview but..." then proceed to fill in the page until you run out of buts.

Asking relevant questions may also help, for instance:

» What meanings could I have created based on my past disappointments?

» What pessimistic thoughts reoccur every time I think about the interview?

» What unnecessary assumptions do I make about the interview?

» How might my standards be affecting my ability to relax?

» Am I holding onto any stereotypical beliefs that are holding me back?

Challenge
Now that we have identified our limiting beliefs, the next step is to challenge them. By challenging our old beliefs, we create doubt. This doubt is all we need to be able to slot a new empowering belief in its place. Strong beliefs are not always easy to destroy. These can, however, be weakened when they are challenged.

» Challenge the beliefs directly
The first way to break down a limiting belief is to question its validity. Challenge yourself to find evidence against it, and build a case that proves the assumption wrong. You could ask yourself questions, such as: How do I know this? Is it impossible or just hard? Is there another way I could look at this? Could there be another truth here?

» Question the source
Do you know where your assumptions came from in the first place? Did you choose these beliefs or are they by-products of someone else's belief systems? Sometimes, realising a belief is not ours is enough to destroy it.

» Challenge their usefulness
During our life, we have picked up beliefs that have not served us or were only valid for a certain period, but we have held onto them ever since. Ask yourself: Does this belief still serve a useful purpose? Does it help me move closer to my goals? Does this belief help or hurt me? If this belief limits me, how can I quickly get rid of it?

» Weigh the consequences
The avoidance of pain is a great motivator, so realising the negative consequences of our beliefs, may provide the motivation we need to destroy it. Ask yourself: What has this belief cost me in the past? If I don't change this belief now, what will the consequences be in the future?

Replace

In this final step, we will identify and install alternative empowering beliefs. To do this, we simply need to reinforce each new belief with sufficient evidence to support it. Ask yourself: What have I done in my past that could contribute as evidence? What activities and actions could I take now that would strengthen this belief?

Keep a journal and continue creating evidence towards it. The more ingrained you can make the belief, the more evidence it will begin to identify for itself, and the deeper rooted the belief will become.

This step isn't an overnight process. It does take time to imprint the belief deeply enough into your subconscious that it will stick long term and overpower the old limiting belief but, with repetition and reinforcement, positive changes will begin to happen in your life.

Use your Imagination

Since our brain knows no difference between real or imagined experiences, it is possible to use mental rehearsal and visualisation techniques to manipulate our physiology and improve our interview performance.

Find a quiet space where you're unlikely to be disturbed for 10-15 minutes and use these basic guidelines:

» Get into a comfortable position and allow your body to relax. Take a few deep breaths and, as you exhale, imagine all of the tension slowly leaving your body.

» Now imagine it is the day of your interview and begin to visualise the entire day, scene by scene, in your subconscious. When running through the events in your mind, imagine feeling relaxed, yet energised as you converse effortlessly with other candidates and the recruiters. Observe how others warm to your friendly and confident nature. Imagine your composure as you intelligently answer the interviewer's questions.

» Make each scene as vivid and real as you can. Bring it closer, make the colours richer, sense the atmosphere in the room, and introduce sounds and feelings. Really intensify the experience.

» When you are pleased with the imagined performance, begin to introduce challenging scenarios for different characters you may encounter, questions you may be asked, and pressure you may be put under.

Using this rehearsal technique for just twenty minutes a day will train your brain to actually perform the new skills and behaviours.

Repetition is the key to success with this technique. The more you practice, the better you will get and the more confident you will feel.

Anchor your State

Anchoring is an NLP (Neuro Linguistic Programming) term which describes a process whereby certain psychological states, positive or negative, become associated with and can be triggered by a certain stimulus.

Using certain techniques, it is possible to anchor positive states so that we can readily access them on demand, or we can break the association of undesirable states using collapsing techniques.

Create an anchor

» Step 1: Identify
To begin the process of creating an anchor, we first need to identify the desirable state. For instance: confidence, calmness, assertiveness.

» Step 2: Locate a memory
Next we need to recall a particular time in our life when we have felt the desired state. The context is unimportant, but the experience must have been a powerful one.

» Step 3: Get into state
With an experience in mind, mentally put yourself back into that experience. Use all your senses to make the experience as vivid and intense as you can. What did you see? What could you hear? Where there any smells present? How did you look? How did you feel? Now really focus in and intensify those feelings.

» Step 4: Anchor the state
When the desired state has been captured and the feeling is about to hit its peak, it is time to anchor those feelings. This is done by firing off a unique combination of cues.

The cue combination can include one which is visual, one auditory, and one kinaesthetic. For example, pinching the skin above your knuckles, while visualising the colour blue, and saying the word 'YES' is a unique cue combination that would be appropriate.

» Step 5: Repeat
To really condition the anchor, repeat this procedure at least five times. The more repetitions, the stronger the anchor will be.

» Step 6: Test
Now that our anchor has been installed, we need to test its effectiveness. To do this, we simply need to fire off our unique cue combination that we set up in step 4.

For best results, break state for a few moments and think of something completely unrelated.

If the anchor has been a success, the desired state should be experienced within 10-15 seconds. If the feeling is not satisfactory, further reinforcement repetitions may be carried out, or the power of anchor stacking may be introduced.

Collapse an anchor

» Step 1: Identify
Before we begin the process of collapsing an anchor, we first need to identify the problem state (e.g. panic, anger, anxiety) and decide an alternative desired state that we would like to create in its place (e.g. confidence, calmness, assertiveness).

» Step 2 : Create
Next, we begin the process of creating anchors (See above). First we will create an anchor for the desirable state we want to capture. Then, we need to repeat the process for the undesirable state we want to collapse.

In creating these two anchors, we want to create the desirable anchor according to the steps outlined previously, however, the undesirable state should be created with less intensity in order to give the positive state more power.

This can be done effectively by simply visualising the negative state in less context, using fewer senses, and only using one kinaesthetic cue (be sure this cue is different to the one selected for the positive anchor)

» Step 3: Repeat
To really condition the anchors, repeat the procedure at least five times. The more repetitions, the stronger the anchor will be.

» Step 4: Test
Now that our anchors have been installed, we need to test their effectiveness. To do this, we simply need to fire off our unique cue combination.

For best results, break state for a few moments and think of something completely unrelated.

If the anchor has been a success, the state should be experienced within 10-15 seconds. If the feeling is not satisfactory, further reinforcement repetitions may be carried out, or the power of anchor stacking may be introduced.

» Step 5: Collapse
Finally, we begin the process of collapsing our problem anchor.

To do this, we simply fire both anchors at the same time. As you do this, your physiology will feel somewhat confused as it tries to achieve both states simultaneously. If the positive anchor has been created strong enough, the negative anchor will begin to clear. At this stage, we can let the negative anchor release, while we continue to fire and hold onto the positive state.

» Step 6: Test
To test the success of the collapse, break state for a few moments and try to re-fire the negative anchor. The result should be neutral. If the state persists the procedure may be repeated, using the power of stacking positive anchors.

Ask Resourceful Questions

When we ask questions of ourselves, we prompt our minds to search our internal memory archive for reasons and/or evidence to support those questions. So, whether we ask an empowering question, such as: "How can I achieve this?' or "Why am I so lucky?" or a disempowering question, such as: "Why does this always happen to me?" or "Why can't I ever get this right?" our brains will work to bring forth answers.

Wouldn't you rather have your brain bring back answers that create happiness and success? Well, why don't you make yourself a commitment to only ask empowering questions of yourself from this point forward? It's simple to do, and will really enhance the quality of your life.

Replace:

» "What's the point? I never pass anyway"
» "I always get nervous in interviews"
» "Why can't I be confident?"

With:

» "What steps can I take that will increase my chances of success?"
» "What can I do to manage my emotions?"
» "How can I feel confident right now?"

Adjust your Physiology

Our physiology has a direct impact on our psyche. Therefore, if we make some simple adjustments to our physiology, we can easily adjust our mood. To illustrate this point more clearly, try the following experiments:

Imagine for a moment that you harbour some self esteem issues and have a serious lack of confidence. Now ask yourself the following questions and then perform the appropriate corresponding movements:

If I were confident...

- » How would I move?
- » How would I sit?
- » How would I sound?
- » How would I look?
- » How would I breathe?
- » What gestures would I make?

Did you notice the change? Now try this:

- » Curl your facial muscles up into a smile. Now, while maintaining this beautiful smile, try to become depressed or angry.

Now, anytime in the future that you find yourself in a negative state, use this technique to deliberately change it. If you feel unconfident, increase your confidence by acting like someone who has an abundance of it. If you feel sad, act like someone that is happy. If you feel tired, become energetic. If you feel angry... and so on.

Make the Swish

The swish pattern is a simple, yet very powerful sub modality technique which enables us to address unwanted and damaging behaviour responses, and replace them with appropriate and empowering ones. In essence, this method reprograms our brains neuro-associations.

For illustrative purposes, let's imagine that in stress provoking situations, such as an interview, we feel compelled to bite our nails. Clearly, this is an unwanted and unhelpful habit which does not create a positive impression. Using the swish method, we can completely and immediately eliminate this bad habit. Here's how we use the swish pattern:

» Step 1: Identify the problem behaviour
First, we need to identify the problem behaviour. This could be one of many common problems such as: Stammering, blushing or trembling. Now, create an image that represents the habit or behaviour.

» Step 2: Identify the desired behaviour
Now identify an alternative behaviour and create a corresponding mental image of this state. For example: In the case of stammering, you may see yourself conversing clearly and effortlessly.

» Step 3: Identify suitable sub modalities
Identify and apply a sub modality that will reduce the desire for the problem behaviour in step 1 (E.g. Use a monochrome, unfocused image) and another that will increase desire for the empowering behaviour in step 2 (E.g. Increase the size, sounds and brightness).

» Step 4: Time to swish
Finally, we will use the swish pattern to replace the problem state. To do this, we will take the problem image from step 1, with the sub modality applied, and place it prominently in our mind.

Next we will take the desired image, also with the sub modality applied, and imagine it being placed into a sling shot. Now, imagine the sling shot drawing the image far into the distance, feel the tension of the elastic. Then, when ready to activate the swish, simply release the image from the sling shot and allow it to come hurtling forwards so that it smashes through the original image.

Allow the image to grow bigger, brighter, and more colourful. Let it completely fill your mind to make it really compelling.

To create even more power, we can include auditory and kinaesthetic cues to the pattern. For instance: we could say "whoosh" or "swish" while throwing a fist into the air.

» Step 5: Repeat
To reinforce the new behaviour, repeat step 4 at least 10 times in quick succession, each time making it faster. To avoid looping and reversing the pattern, it is important to break state between each cycle so that we always begin from and break through the starting image.

Find your Focus

What we focus on has a direct impact on how we feel and what we experience. So, when we focus on what we don't want, such as 'not feeling stressed' and 'not feeling unconfident' we only serve to attract more of these feelings because we are focusing all of our attention on them. Rather, we should focus on what we do want.

For instance:

Instead of:	Focus on:
Don't feel stressed	Feel calm and relaxed
Don't feel anxious	Feel alert and confident
Don't be upset	Feel joyful

Create Compelling Reasons

There may be challenging periods that arise during your interview which cause you to question your motives. If you have compelling reasons for wanting the job, your conviction will give you the driving force you need to carry you through these challenging moments.

So, ask yourself:

» Why do I really want this job?

» How will this job change my life?

» How will I feel when I am successful?

» What would I enjoy about the job?

Affirm & Incant

Affirmations and incantations are used to promote positive changes in our life.

Affirmations are short positive statements which are repeated several times in order to impress on our subconscious mind. To perform an affirmation, we simply take our chosen statement, for example "I am confident and successful in everything I do", and repeat it several times in quick succession with all the conviction and passion we can muster.

An incantation is a supercharged affirmation which also engages our physiology. This action of getting our body involved creates a much more powerful outcome.

Common Concerns

Unless there is some form of medical condition present, each of the common concerns listed below are generally symptoms of an underlying psychological element, such as anxiety. If these symptoms are psychologically driven, using the techniques described within this session will help manage, and even eliminate, these symptoms. However, there are specific techniques that can be used to minimise their impact.

Challenge: Anxiety
Nervous feelings before an interview are quite legitimate and most people can relate to feeling tense or fearful on the run up to such an event. In fact, a little interview anxiety can make us more alert and really enhance our performance, so we would never want to completely eliminate interview anxiety. However, when that anxiety becomes strong enough to negatively affect our clarity of thought and dialogue, some anxiety management techniques should be introduced.

» Proper preparation
   Anxiety can be the result of poor preparation. If you anticipate potential questions, prepare appropriate answers, research the airline and understand the requirements of the job, you will be better mentally prepared. If your mind is prepared, it makes sense that you will feel calmer, and more confident in yourself and your ability to handle the interview.

» Deep breathing
   Deep breathing will steady your rapid heartbeat, strengthen your shallow breathing, provide your brain with vital oxygen and make you more alert.

   Technique: Find a comfortable seating or standing position. Now, over the count of seven, inhale slowly and deeply through your nose. You should notice your stomach expand as your lungs begin to fill with oxygen.

   Now, over the count of 10-13 seconds, begin to exhale slowly through your mouth, allowing your stomach to gradually flatten. As you release the oxygen from your lungs allow your shoulders to relax and feel the tension release.

   Continue this pattern of in and out breaths until your breathing becomes steady and the anxiety subsides.

» Remediation
Hypnotherapy, Cognitive Behavioural Therapy (CBT) and Neuro Linguistic Programming (NLP) sessions are very effective at dealing with deep rooted anxiety issues.

» Medication
If you find your anxiety levels quite literally overwhelm you at interviews, you may be considering medication. While this is a method I don't advocate, there are over the counter supplements, such as Kalms, St John's Wort, and Bachs Rescue Remedy, which can really help take the edge off anxiety. Otherwise, stronger prescription medications such as Xanex or Beta Blockers may be prescribed by your medical practitioner.

Challenge: Sweating

» Dress Colours
Black, navy and pure white will help disguise sweat marks, as will the camouflaging nature of patterns. Avoid: Light colours such as pale blue or grey.

» Dress Fabrics
Wear breathable fabrics such as: 100% cotton, pima cotton, seersucker, linen, 100% wool, merino, and cashmere. Avoid: Corduroy, flannel, silk, polyester and polyester blends, nylon, and acetate

» Dress Style
Wear loose fitting over and under garments for maximum air flow. Add layers, such as a suit jacket, waistcoat or cardigan, to disguise sweating.

» Antiperspirant
Use a clear, unperfumed antiperspirant. Beware: Antiperspirant can leave a film residue on your clothing. To avoid these stains, allow the antiperspirant to dry completely before putting on your shirt.

» Keep fresh
During bathroom breaks, wash your hands with lukewarm water. Blot your hands dry with a tissue and finish off with a light mist of a clear antiperspirant. Avoid: Cold or hot water, air dryers and sticky antiperspirants.

» Seek medical advice
Individuals with Hyperhidrosis, may seek the advice of a medical professional or dermatologist. Both can advise and prescribe suitable treatments, such as: Prescription strength antiperspirants and Botox.

Challenge: Not Enough Eye Contact
Good eye contact is one of the most important factors of body language. Shifty eyes, or complete avoidance of contact can suggest dishonesty, rudeness or lack of confidence. If you find eye contact anxiety provoking and uncomfortable, the following techniques will certainly help.

» Use a mirror
Practice your eye contact by using your own mirrored image as a guinea pig. When you see yourself in the mirror every day, make a point of looking directly into your own eyes.

» Fake it
Rather than look directly into the eyes, you can fake it by either directing your gaze at their eyebrows, forehead, or bridge of the nose. This is not a permanent solution by any means, but it will certainly ease you into the process.

» Avoid staring
In an attempt to forge eye contact, we may begin to stare. This can indicate aggression and make others feel uncomfortable. To avoid this extreme, lighten your gaze and keep it friendly. This can be achieved by allowing your eyes to go slightly out of focus.

» Use opportunities
If you have notes, you can temporarily break eye contact as you refer to these. Also, f there is a second recruitment officer present, this will give you another opportunity to break eye contact as you periodically direct your focus back and forth between the two.

Challenge: Blanking out
Even with all the preparation in the world, our mind can betray us and draw a blank at the most inopportune moment. If this happens, take a deep breath, remain composed and employ some of the following techniques:

» Refer to your résumé
Your résumé provides an immediate memory jog in these instances, so refer to it as and when necessary. You may also want to jot down some key words or phrases inside a professional looking notebook beforehand.

» Wait a moment
You don't have to always answer questions immediately. It is perfectly permissible to pause and collect your thoughts before proceeding with a response. In fact, taking the time to think through your response can make you appear deliberate and thoughtful. Answering without regard for your answer can make you look impulsive.

» Be honest
If you don't have relative experience in a particular area, or simply don't know the answer, you need to be honest and say so. At this point, you could offer an alternative piece of information.

» Stall
If you feel you can get away with it, reflect the question back to allow yourself a little more thinking time.

» Stay composed
Some recruiters will purposely throw in some curve ball questions to see how you react to pressure and think on your feet. In these cases, the interviewer is probably more interested in observing your reaction than they are about the answer you provide. So, stay calm and do your best to answer in a confident manner. In the worst case, simply be honest and admit you don't know the answer.

Challenge: Cotton mouth

» Keep fully hydrated by drinking plenty of water on the run up to the event. Fill up on water during breaks and periodically sip on water throughout the assessment.

» Stimulate saliva flow by adding a splash of lemon juice to your water bottle, sucking on sugar free candy or chewing sugarless gum. Gently biting your tongue can also activate the glands that stimulate saliva flow.

» Avoid salty and sugary foods, alcohol (including alcohol based mouthwash), caffeinated beverages and tobacco products as these inhibit saliva flow and dry the mouth out.

Challenge: Involuntary facial motions
Unless there is a medical condition present, involuntary facial twitching and trembling are generally ensuing of overly stressed muscles, such as forced smiling. These distressing symptoms are especially pronounced during an interview when we feel compelled to smile, or are attempting to conceal our nerves. To gain relief from these symptoms, we simply need to control how and when we smile.

Maintaining a constant grin is not only unnecessary and uncomfortable, it will also look insincere. Gentle and understated smiles are more than appropriate for prolonged periods, and full toothed smiles should be reserved for introductions and the occasional injection during conversation.

Next time you feel your facial muscles begin to tense, try relaxing your smile and see what a difference it makes.

Challenge: Fidgeting
Fidgeting, tapping and excessive gesturing with give the appearance of uncertainty, nervousness and unpreparedness. To effectively manage these movements, use the techniques outlined below.

» Identify
  If you are unsure of any habits you may have, ask a friend, partner or coworker for their views. Alternatively, record yourself in a short mock interview and examine the footage. Mark down any ineffective mannerisms you can identify (playing with your pen, drumming your fingers, touching your face or hair, clearing your throat, or rubbing your nose) and then begin the process of eliminating each of them.

» Beware of props
  Props can easily exaggerate any fidgeting, so if you have a pen, résumé or bag with you, avoid fiddling with them. Be equally mindful of jewellery, such as twirling earrings or a finger ring.

» Mind your hands
  If the movements you employ are subtle, it is perfectly okay to gesture your arms and hands to endorse your words. Subtle means, keeping the movements below shoulder height and above the waist. If you find your movements become excessive or distracting, simply intertwine your fingers and rest your hands on the table or clasped loosely in your lap.

Challenge: Perceived Arrogance
Sometimes, a high level of confidence may be misconstrued as arrogance. If you feel you are sometimes wrongly labelled as arrogant, the following guidelines will help you maintain your confidence, while avoiding this assumption.

» Be open
  We all have weaknesses, to say otherwise will certainly make you appear arrogant. Be clear about what you do and don't know, and be prepared to listen and learn from others.

» Be humble
Act with humility when you are recognised for a job well done. Acknowledge the effort of others by sharing and giving praise where appropriate, and be accountable when errors transpire.

» Be approachable
To make yourself appear more approachable, use open and inviting body language, and adopt a warm, friendly expression. Inject some personality into your conversations, make good use of eye contact (see above) and remember to use peoples names.

» Be considerate
Genuinely acknowledge and compliment the hard work and efforts of others. Listen to and respect others opinions, and avoid interrupting when others are speaking.

Challenge: Blushing

Go green

» A purposeful green pigmented concealer or foundation will minimise the impact of redness.

Seek medical advice

» Blushing which is caused by a medical condition should be treated by a medical professional. Prescription medication may be prescribed.

Challenge: Vocal paralysis

Under severe pressure, our voice may become partially paralysed. The physical symptoms of this may include stuttering, a weak and shaky vocal tone, or an unusually high pitch. These symptoms can be managed by adopting the following techniques:

» Speak in shorter phrases

» Slow your pace

» Control your breathing by using steady in-out breaths

» Maintain an upright posture

» Ignore the symptoms until they naturally relieve themselves

» Seek the assistance of a vocal coach

Invent your Introduction

First impressions are absolutely critical for interview success. The impression you provide within the first few minutes will be the one that sticks and, anything following, will become merely a confirmation of that first impression. So, to assist you in getting off to the very best start, I have devised some tips that will make you appear confident, friendly, relaxed and professional.

On arrival

Upon arriving at the venue, approach the reception desk and introduce yourself, your purpose and whom you are expecting to meet. For example:

> "Hello. My name is Jane Doe and I'm here for an interview with Carrie Loren"

Once signed in, thank the receptionist and take a seat in the waiting area.

Meeting the candidates

If you are attending an open day or group selection process where other candidates will be present, you will have many introductions to contend with. These introductions are just as important as any other and must not be underestimated.

Candidate introductions should be handled in much the same way as any other, however, you may keep these slightly less formal if you wish. As you approach the candidate(s), smile and make eye contact, then say hello and introduce yourself. In a one to one introduction, offer a handshake if you so desire. In a group introduction, a handshake is unnecessary. If the candidate(s) responds positively to your approach, you may engage in further small talk.

Meeting the recruiter(s)

When you meet each recruiter for the first time, be sure to stand up straight, make eye contact and smile. Then, allow the recruiter to initiate the introduction and the handshake.

» If they greet you by name, your response should be:
  "Hello Ms. Loren. It's a pleasure to meet you".

» If an introduction is needed, simply say:
  "I'm Jane Doe. It's a pleasure to meet you" or
  "Hello Ms. Loren. Pleased to meet you. I'm Jane Doe"

At this stage, pleasantries may be initiated by the recruiter as a way to break the ice. Just follow their lead and go with the flow.

03:00

Polish your image

> "A strong, positive self image is the best possible preparation for success"
>
> **- Joyce Brothers**

During the first few minutes of the interview, the recruitement team will make certain judgements about a candidates character and suitability based on their appearance. Thus, if we are to succeed in creating that all important positive first impression, it is essential that we make a valid effort to present a polished and conservative image.

Organise your Outfit

Business casual may be perfectly acceptable for some airlines and it is the very least that should be considered. For maximum impact, however, classic business attire is a safe choice that will give a clean, polished and professional appearance.

Here are some guidelines that you need to pay attention to:

» Fit:
Wear clothing that fits your body correctly. Clothing that is too short or too long, too big or too small is never a good look.

» Suitability:
Even if you opt for a casual look, your attire needs to be suitable. Too much cleavage, exposed midriffs, and excessively short skirts are not suitable, so don't do it.

» Patterns:
Some patterns can appear overwhelming, so play it safe with a solid colour or stick to conservative and subtle patterns such as pinstripes.

» Colours:
Too much colour can also be overwhelming, so wear traditional colours, such as: navy blue, charcoal grey and black, and introduce colour sparingly and subtly through your shirt/blouse or tie. This will give your outfit a professional, yet unique character.

» Fabric:
Some fabrics wrinkle easily, so look for a suit that is made of a wrinkle resistant fabric such as wool.

Whatever style of dress you ultimately choose, you must feel comfortable and confident.

Tend to your Grooming

» Hands & Nails
Ensure that your nails are clean, neatly trimmed and reasonable in length. Nail polish should be conservative and match in colour. Avoid charms, glitter and multicoloured polish.

» Cosmetics
Use cosmetics to conceal blemishes and enhance your assets but avoid going over the top. Less is more in a formal interview setting where a natural and polished look will be appreciated.

» Hair
Hair should be neat and well groomed, and outrageous colours or styles should be avoided. Frizzy or loose ends can appear messy so should be brushed into place and fixed, but be careful not to produce a slicked down appearance.

Male cabin crew are not normally permitted to have beards so a cleanly shaven or closely trimmed style is recommended.

Accessorize

» Perfume & Cologne
If you choose to wear perfume or cologne, select a light scent and wear it sparingly.

» Jewellery
Keep jewellery minimal and conservative. Wear no more than one ring per hand and avoid oversized pieces.

» Watch
Wear a simple working watch which doesn't beep.

» Portfolio
Consider carrying a small leather portfolio rather than a briefcase or everyday handbag. Portfolios are simple, organised and easy to carry.

» Tattoos & Facial Piercings
Visible tattoos and facial piercings are not acceptable. Tattoos will need to be concealed and piercings. removed.

04:00

The Final Countdown

"If you do what you've always done, you'll get what you've always gotten"

- Anthony Robbins

The Run Up

» Rehearse
On the final run up to the event, set aside some time to go through a final rehearsal of your presentation. Practice answering questions and going over talking points with a friend or relative and use this opportunity to iron out any wrinkles.

» Perform a dry run
If possible, take the opportunity to visit the venue in advance. This dry run will familiarise you with the route, parking and travel time and allow you to avoid becoming lost or late on the day. If you can do the route at the same time of day, you'll benefit from the added simulation of traffic and road conditions.

If you are unable to make an advance visit the venue, use the internet to map out a detailed route map that also provides distance and time estimations.

» Inspect your outfit
A few days before the event, take out the outfit you plan to wear and make sure it is clean, pressed, and has no buttons missing. Have it dry cleaned and repaired if necessary.

» Get a hair cut
Consider having your hair cut a week out from the day. This will allow the cut to soften slightly for a more natural look, while still retaining some of the freshness of the cut.

» Calm your nerves
If you feel your anxiety levels begin to escalate, put aside time to practice the strategies outlined in this book.

The Evening Before

» Review your résumé
As you complete a final review of your résumé, notice and take pride in your listed achievements. Take the time to remind yourself of why you want the job and what you have to offer.

» Check travel arrangements
If travelling by car, make sure the tank has plenty of petrol and that you have change available for parking meters. If using public transport, check timetables.

» Prepare your outfit
Take out the outfit you plan to wear and go through a final inspection to make sure it is clean and pressed. Inspect your hosiery for runs or holes. Clean and polish your shoes. Prepare your accessories and gather your portfolio pieces. Then, lay the pieces out ready for the morning.

» Organise your portfolio
To avoid a morning rush, prepare your portfolio in advance.

» Get an early night
To ensure you are fresh and alert, you'll need a good night's sleep. So, aim to retire no later than 11 pm. A warm aromatherapy bath before bed will help you relax and unwind.

» Set your alarm
Before winding down for the night, ensure your alarm is set to the appropriate time. For caution, you may set two alarms or enlist a relative to give you a friendly wake up call.

On the Day

» Drink a glass of water
As soon as you rise, rehydrate and wake up your system with a large glass of water.

» Stretch
Incorporating a full body stretch into your morning routine will increase blood flow and wake up your tired muscles.

» Psyche yourself up
Jump start your motivation by chanting your incantations, acknowledging your goals and visualising your success.

» Listen to music
Listening to your favourite upbeat music is a great way to put you in a good mood. It will lighten the atmosphere and increase your energy level.

» Eat a good breakfast
Oatmeal is light, natural and slow releasing so it will provide ample energy for the day. Perhaps combine it with a protein shake and piece of fruit for a power breakfast.

» Leave with plenty of time to spare
Arriving late to an interview means you immediately start the interview from behind the rest of the candidates. You also risk arriving in a panic. You should, therefore, aim to arrive at least 15 minutes early and allow extra travelling time to account for any unforeseen delays.

It is better to be an hour early than it is to be just a minute late. You can always grab a coffee and go through your notes.

On Arrival

» Freshen up
If you have time, and it's convenient to do so, take a moment when you arrive to freshen up. Inspect your outfit, wash your hands, touch up your makeup, pop in a breath mint and spritz some deodorant. Be sure to discard any gum or breath mints before you enter the announce your arrival.

» Turn off your cell phone
To avoid potential interruptions, turn off your cell phone or put it on silent mode as soon as you arrive.

Portfolio Essentials

Documentation

- » Copies of your résumé
- » Interview invitation
- » A copy of your application form
- » Passport
- » Certificates
- » Reference details

Photographs
You should take one full length with one or two passport sized.

A notepad
A notepad is tidier than lots of pieces of paper.

2 pens
With two pens, you will have a backup if the first runs out of ink or becomes lost. Alternatively, you can lend one to another candidate.

A pencil and eraser
These two items are a must as they will make any mistakes easy to rectify.

Part 2

Apply

"Don't worry about failures. Worry about the
opportunities you miss when you don't even try"

- Jack Canfield

05:00

Pass the telephone Screening

"A successful man is one who can lay a firm foundation with bricks others have thrown at him"

- David Brinkley

In a quest to save time and money, some airlines are now adopting telephone screening techniques. The telephone screening allows selectors to determine a candidate's eligibility, and then eliminate unsuitable candidates without going to the expense of inviting them to attend an interview.

The information you supply at this stage is vital to your continuation in the process so you need to be prepared. Thus, I have devised the following guidelines to give you the best chance of success.

Format

Telephone screenings vary between airlines and, generally, come in two formats:

» Quick and general
  This style of screening is usually straightforward and consists of a series of simple questions which seek to identify eligibility. For example: Are you over xx" in height?, Are you over xx years old? Do you have customer service experience?

» Deep and detailed
  This format is more comparable to a formal interview and you can expect tougher elimination questions. For example: Why do you want to work for us? Why do you want to be cabin crew? Tell me about your weaknesses?

Be Prepared

As soon as you submit a résumé or application form, you should be prepared to receive a call from a recruiter, at any time. Although you cannot control the timing of these calls, there are some precautions you can take to ensure that you are not caught completely off guard.

Outgoing voice mail
For times when you are unable to take a call, a professional outgoing voice mail message will provide the best impression. For example:

> "Hello. You have reached Jane Doe's voice mail. I'm sorry I am unable to take your call at present, but please leave your name, telephone number and a short message, and I'll be sure to return your call as soon as possible".

Mobile telephone usage
Where possible, your first choice of contact should be via a land-line telephone. If a mobile phone is unavoidable, however, make sure it has a clear sound and you maintain a full battery.

Prepare for potential questions
To ensure that you can provide precise answers to the recruiter's questions, you should have your résumé in front of you.

Some questions you might expect in a telephone screening are:

» Can you tell me about yourself and your work history?

» Why are you leaving your present job?

» Why do you want to work for us?

» What interests you about this job?

» What skills can you bring to the position?

You should also be ready to provide some specific examples of accomplishments and experiences which showcase your customer service and teamwork skills.

Take notes
Keep a pen and paper on hand so that you can write down brief notes about the call, including the callers name and phone number.

If you are offered to attend a formal interview, make a note of the date and time, the location and phone number, and directions to the venue (if offered).

Keep hydrated
Depending on the length of the conversation, and how nervous you become, a dry mouth and throat can become a hazard. For this reason, I would suggest sipping on a glass of water throughout the telephone call.

Make a Good Impression

Returning missed calls
Return missed calls promptly and be prepared to interview immediately.

If you reach the recruiter's voice mail, you should leave a message using the following guidelines:

» Speak slowly and clearly
It goes without saying that the recipient should hear and understand every word.

» Avoid filler words
Filler words, such as ums and ahs, sound unprofessional. Avoid their use by preparing your message in advance.

» Introduce yourself
Begin the message by introducing yourself and identifying for who the message is for. Example: "Hello. This is a message from Jane Doe for Carrie Loren"

» Leave a short summary message
A short summary detailing your reason for calling is sufficient, such as: "I received your message regarding the cabin crew selection interview and would be eager to discuss the position with you further"

» Close the message
End the call by stating your availability and telephone number(s). For instance: "You can reach me on 01137 483 948 Monday to Friday between 9 and 5, or on my mobile 07897 786 897 from 5 onwards. I look forward to speaking with you shortly".

Speak Clearly
Make a conscious effort to slow the pace of your speech and enunciate clearly. Speaking too fast, too close to the mouthpiece or mumbling will make you harder to understand.

Use Silence
It is easy to talk too much when you are nervous. A moment of silence, while it might seem awkward to you, lets the recruiter know that you are done.

Use the recruiter's name
To establish rapport, write down the recruiter's name and use it throughout the conversation.

Dress the part
If you are initiating the call, or if you know to expect one, you should make an effort to dress appropriately. This doesn't necessarily mean full business attire, but it does mean something that will make you feel relaxed, yet alert and businesslike. Slacks or a bathrobe will hardly make you feel professional, and it certainly won't put you in the correct frame of mind for a formal telephone conversation.

Keep an upright posture
To give your voice more energy and projection power, try maintaining a good upright posture.

Pay attention to your tone
Your voice plays a key role in sending the correct messages. If your tone sounds bored and distracted, it won't matter how enthusiastically you phrase your answers because your tone will be the message that sticks with the recruiter. The key is to match the sound of your voice to the words you are using.

To check the level of enthusiasm in your voice, you can practice with a tape recorder.

Ask for clarification
If you are unsure or feel you have misunderstood a question, it is better to request the recruiter to repeat, rephrase or summarise the question than to answer the question incorrectly.

Rather than jump straight in with your question, though, you should consider using a polite introductory phrase, such as:

- » I beg your pardon, but I don't quite follow/understand. I wonder if you could rephrase that in a different way?

- » Do you think you could repeat the part about ... once again please?

- » Pardon me. Would you mind repeating that?

- » Sorry, but I'm not sure I'm following you.

- » Let's see if I understand/understood you correctly ...

- » Do you/Does this mean that...
- » Would it be correct to say that...
- » So in other words...

Verbal Cues
Although you should never interrupt the recruiter, you shouldn't listen in total silence either. Instead, use verbal feedback cues to indicate that you are listening and that you understand. This will encourage the recruiter to continue.

Some verbal feedback signals include:

- » "uh huh"
- » "I see."
- » "Yes"
- » "Ok"
- » "I understand"
- » "That's interesting"
- » "Sure"
- » "Right"
- » "Of course"

Smile
A smile will add warmth to your voice and make it sound friendly, inviting and enthusiastic. To give yourself a boost, there are several things you can do:

- » Keep a humorous, inspirational or special picture nearby
- » Keep a mirror in front of you as a reminder to smile
- » Think about someone you care about
- » Have a funny joke pinned up
- » Have some happy music playing in the background (make sure it is appropriate music though and not too loud)

Faux Pas Alerts

Leading or controlling

Don't try to lead or control the conversation, this is the recruitment officer's Job. You can, however, ask questions of your own when opportunities arise.

Distractions & Interruptions

Minimise potential distractions by taking the call in a quiet room. If you are caught at an inopportune time, politely ask the caller to hold for a brief moment while you move to a quiet location. You could say "Could you give me a moment to go to a room where we won't be interrupted?"

Alternatively, if the timing is really bad, you can respectfully request an alternative date and time by saying "I do apologise, but is there a time I can reach you later? I'm very interested in the position and want to give you my undivided attention, but I'm afraid that now isn't the best time."

Interrupting the recruiter

Unless absolutely necessary, you should never interrupt the recruiter while they are speaking. Write down any questions or comments you have for later.

Umm, Anyways

Anyways, you know how when you are, like, really nervous, and you ,ummm, find it hard to verbalise and stuff and you say silly things that, kind of, make you sound, like, kind of, unprofessional and maybe, like, inarticulate?

The useless and annoying verbal mannerisms used in the above example "you know," "like," "in other words," "kind of," "ummm," and "anyways." should be avoided at all costs. Besides making you sound unprofessional, they also detract attention from your message.

Unprepared or unnecessary questions

To stand out as an informed and competent applicant, your questions should reflect that you have researched the airline and the position. Asking questions that have already been addressed within the airline's literature will make you appear unprepared and incompetent.

Likewise, asking questions that are based on money and benefits will make you appear selfishly motivated and give a negative impression about your motives for the position and/or the airline.

Negativity
There is no room for negativity when it comes to interviews of any kind. Be especially careful when discussing other jobs, airlines, people, previous employers and your current job.

Puff Puff, Slurp Slurp
Any sounds you make close to the receiver will be amplified at the other end so avoid smoking, eating and drinking close to the mouthpiece.

Making a Successful Close

As the recruitment officer begins to conclude the interview thank him or her for their time and, if they haven't suggested an in person interview, enquire about the next steps and tell them that you are available for a face-to-face interview.

For example: "I've really enjoyed talking to you and am very interested in the position. What are the next steps in the hiring process? Should I expect to hear from you soon?"

06:00

Produce Polished Photographs

"Don't aim for success if you want it; just do what you love and believe in, and it will come naturally"

- David Frost

The requisition of photographs is so much more than a simple vanity requirement, and I cannot emphasise their importance enough. Not only will your photographs be the recruiter's first impression of you, they will also serve as a visual reminder for the recruiters to refer back to throughout the assessment process, and when making hiring decisions.

By following the simple guidelines that follow, you can be sure that your photos will make a positive and memorable impression.

Requirements

Each airline will have its own specific requirements, and these will be advised when you apply. For reference, though, you can expect the minimum requisition of a head and shoulder shot, generally in the form of a 45 x 35 mm passport photograph. This may also be accompanied by a request for a full length shot, which is subject to varying specifications.

Formal vs Informal

Casual shots, while acceptable for some airlines, carry the risk of appearing sloppy, unprofessional, and inappropriate. As a result, they present a much higher risk of rejection. Business attire, on the other hand, will give the appearance of professionalism, and it is highly unlikely that they will be rejected.

Set the Scene

A solid backdrop will produce a clean and uncluttered appearance. If possible, use a contrasting colour to avoid blending into the surroundings. White or pastel shades usually suit this purpose well.

Work the Angles

Being aware of your most flattering angles and knowing how to use them in front of the camera will make you appear photogenic. Try experimenting with a digital camera. With shots taken from different angles, it will quickly become obvious which angles are the most flattering for you.

Dress the Part

Whatever style of dress you ultimately choose, whether formal or informal, you need to pay attention to:

» Fit:
  Wear clothing that fits your body correctly. Clothing that is too short or too long, too big or too small is never a good look.

» Suitability:
  Even if you opt for a casual look, your attire needs to be suitable. Too much cleavage, exposed midriffs, and excessively short skirts are not suitable, so don't do it.

» Patterns:
Some patterns, such as stripes, can have a negative impact on your photos. Horizontal stripes have a tendency to overwhelm and make you look wide, while closely spaced stripes can create weird effects.

» Colours:
Colours, such as black, red and white can cause difficulties with digital cameras and should be worn with caution.

Recommended styles:

» Women:
Business attire can be as casual as a reasonable length skirt or tailored trousers combined with a blouse, or cardigan/sweater combination, or as smart as a matching dress and jacket set.

» Gents:
A collared shirt and trouser combination is acceptable, with a jacket or blazer being optionally added to complete the look.

Tend to your Grooming

Photographs tend to exaggerate complexion issues and flatten your features. Use cosmetics to re-enhance your features, cover blemishes and create an overall polished look. Pay particular attention to the following:

» Balance your assets:
Use colour to emphasise your cheeks, lips and eyes, but be sure to experiment beforehand as colours can appear more intense in photos.

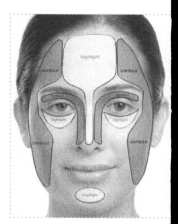

Contouring and highlighting is a clever technique that can be used to create depth, balance your face shape, play down flaws, and emphasise assets. Contouring uses a dark shade and is used to recede areas, while highlighting uses a light shade and is used to protrude areas.

» Control shine:
It is important to control the shine, particularly around the t-zone area (nose and forehead), as this will reflect strongly in photos. For minor shine issues, a powder foundation should do the trick. For more problematic skin, an oil absorbing moisturiser or oil balancing gel may be more suitable.

» Counter redness:
Redness will stand out in photos. If the redness is minimal, a standard foundation should suffice. If you suffer from troublesome redness, a more purposeful green coloured concealer or foundation will certainly minimise the impact to a much higher degree. Use these with caution, though, as they are very heavy duty and can give your skin an excessively pale look.

» Conceal blemishes:
Use concealer or foundation to conceal blemishes such as spots, under eye circles and scars.

» Refresh your eyes:
Eye drops will make your eyes glisten, and clear any redness.

Your hair should be neat and well groomed, and outrageous colours or styles should be avoided.. Frizzy or loose ends can appear messy so should be brushed into place and fixed, but be careful not to produce a slicked down appearance.

Warm your Smile

A warm and sincere smile will complete the look, but creating a beautiful smile on demand is a learned skill which needs to be practiced.

The fake smile, aptly named the 'Pan-Am Smile' because of the flight attendants of Pan-American Airlines, is simply a courtesy smile that will not translate well in your photos. A 'Duchenne Smile', on the other hand, will provide the most beautiful and sincere looking smile, and this is the smile we are looking to achieve.

Here are some tips that will assist you in generating your photo perfect smile.

Produce a natural smile

The most beautiful smiles are the ones that are natural. If you are using a professional photographer, they will be skilled at drawing out your natural smile, but if you are using an unskilled family member, you will need to channel some of your inner happiness. This can be achieved by thinking of a genuine reason to smile, such as recalling a happy memory, looking at a silly picture, or remembering a good joke.

Fake it till you make it

When it is simply impossible to summons a genuine smile, you will need to fake it. Here's some guidelines that will help.

Pan-Am Smile

» Time it right:
The secret to producing a relaxed and natural smile is to time it so that you don't have to hold it for too long. Try looking away from the camera, then just before the photograph is taken, face the camera and smile.

» Use your eyes:
Smiling eyes are required to complete the look. To achieve this effect, imagine the camera is someone you really fancy. Raise your eyebrows and cheekbones a little, and slightly squint the corners of your eyes. Notice the amazing transformation this creates.

Duchenne Smile

Copyright Paul Ekman 2003,
"Emotions Revealed," Owl Books, 2007

07:00

Create a Compelling Resume/CV

"Action is the foundational key to all success"

- Pablo Picasso

First and foremost, a résumé is used to enable employers to screen out unsuitable candidates. If successful through this initial screening stage, it will then be used to formulate suitable questions for the interview.

Because the recruiters will have no information about you beyond this document, it will be a major influence in the nature and direction of the interview. This allows an element of predictability and makes it a very powerful document indeed.

With such a valuable tool at your disposal, it is important that it represents the best you have to offer. If your résumé is strong, it will focus the recruiter's questioning on information that presents your image strongly. The following guidelines will help you achieve this.

OCR Technology

To facilitate more efficient processing of résumés, some larger airlines use a computerised tracking system. This system uses OCR (Optical Character Recognition) technology whereby incoming résumés are scanned as a graphic image, converted back into text, read and added to the database.

With this in mind, it is important to write and format your résumé in such a way that it can be successfully processed by these sophisticated systems. In this instance, the following guidelines apply:

Formatting

Simple formatting will yield the best results. So, avoid unnecessary and unreliable formatting such as italics, shading, and fancy fonts and stick to a simple one column, table less design using a standard typeface such as Georgia, Arial or Verdana.

Keywords

The system scans your résumé for keywords that indicate your skills, qualifications and experience. Following the scan, a score will be awarded based on the number of 'hits'. From this score, the system will either generate a letter of invitation, or a letter of rejection.

To ensure a high score, and an invitation letter, it is essential that you learn and inject as many keywords as possible throughout your resume. The following highlighted keywords are the most widely scanned for:

- » Good **communication** and **interpersonal** skills
- » A **confident** and **friendly** personality
- » Extensive **customer** service experience
- » **Confidence** in dealing with a range of **people**
- » The ability to work effectively in a **team**
- » **Numeracy** skills for handling transactions
- » Ability to handle **difficult customers** firmly and politely
- » Ability to stay **calm**, **composed** and **focused** under **pressure**
- » The ability to be **tactful** and **diplomatic**, but also **assertive** when necessary

Format

There are three basic résumé formats:

- » Chronological:
  The chronological résumé highlights the dates, places of employment and job titles, and is most effective for candidates who have a strong, solid work history. It is less effective for those who want to disguise gaps in employment or frequent job changes.

» Functional:
A functional résumé focuses on skills and experience rather than work history. Its ability to accentuate your transferable skills and detract attention from your career history makes it better suited to those who want to downplay an extreme career change or a chequered employment history. This style is less useful if you have limited work experience as there will be little to highlight.

» Combination:
The combination résumé, as the name implies, is a combination of the chronological and functional formats. It highlights both your work history and your transferable skills, and is most effective when you have a great deal of transferable skills and a solid work history.

The chronological format is most preferred by employers, followed closely by the combination format. The functional format is the least effective.

Outline

For the purpose of a cabin crew position, I have listed possible résumé sections below, in suggested order:

Applicant Information
At the beginning of the résumé, include your name, your home mailing address, your telephone number(s), and your e-mail address. If you have both temporary and permanent addresses, include them both.

Objective Statement (Optional)
An objective is a short statement which defines your career goals. It gives your résumé focus and shows that you have given consideration to your career direction.

Examples: Seeking to utilise extensive customer service experience and exceptional communicative ability within a cabin crew role.

Seeking to pursue a cabin crew position with an airline that rewards commitment and hard work, and offers opportunities to progress.

Key Skills (Optional)
The key skills section provides a fantastic opportunity for you to quickly express your suitability for the role and show what transferable skills your will bring to the position. Additionally, it will bulk out your résumé with the keywords needed for OCR scanning technology.

Key skills to consider are: Communication Skills
                                  Interpersonal Ability
                                  Customer Focus
                                  Team Player
                                  Problem Solver
                                  Leadership

Employment History (Chronological & Combination Formats)
Your employment history should be displayed in reverse chronological order, that is starting with your most recent position and working backwards, and include: the name of the organisation, the position held, the period of employment, the duties performed and results achieved.

The period of employment should include both the start and end dates, and can consist of only the month and year.
When describing your duties use action phrases, rather than compete sentences or generic job descriptions, and list any accomplishments which back up any key skill statements that you have made. For example, if you have stated 'extensive leadership experience' you can use a short action statement such as: "Supervised and trained a team of four junior-level stylists". Three to five of these statements are ideal.

If some entries are more relevant to the cabin crew position, emphasise these and provide only summaries for those of less significance.

Education Summary
Starting with the most recent and working backwards, include the schools/colleges/universities you have attended. Within each entry, include the year of completion ("In progress" or "expected" are acceptable, if necessary) and award(s) you achieved.

Certifications (Optional)
If you have attended any formal certification courses, e.g., First aid, life saving, then list the details here noting the institution name, date and certification awarded.

Activities and Interests (Optional)
Recreational interests reveal a great deal about your personality and create depth to your character. They also serve as excellent sources of additional skills and experiences, which can be advantageous if you lack certain skills and/or experience.

Generalised list statements such as: 'reading, watching television, sport and socialising' are not only bland, they are also too common. Additionally, a statement such as: 'I enjoy spending time with my mates, hitting the town and going out on the razz" lacks variety, doesn't highlight any key skills, and sounds very unprofessional.

Instead, use something such as: 'I have been a keen footballer for as long as I can remember and am an active member of Anytown women's football club where I have been captain of the team for 3 years. I have an active interest in nature, and regularly get involved with and manage conservation assignments. To relax, I attend yoga and meditation classes, which help to keep me focused and relieve stress.'

This statement gives an immediate impression of someone who is balanced and committed. Their interests highlight several admirable qualities such as team spirit and leadership, and it also details their methods of stress management. A recruitment officer would form a positive impression of the candidate based on a statement such as this.

Languages
If you have more than one language ability, indicate whether you speak, read, and/or write the language, and include the level to which you are proficient, such as: native, fluent, proficient or basic conversational ability.

References
Unless specifically requested, the inclusion of reference information is completely optional.

When listing your references, be sure to include: Name, title, professional relationship to you (e.g., Supervisor, manager, and team leader), telephone number and mailing address.

If you decide not to include details, a simple statement such as "References are available on request" is sufficient.

Jane Doe

Seeking to pursue
a cabin crew position
with an airline
that rewards
commitment and
hard work, and
offers opportunities
to progress.

Key Skills

Communication Skills
Exhibits exceptional written and verbal communication skills, and is adept at communicating effectively with people at all levels, and in a manner appropriate to the audience.

Interpersonal Ability
Unsurpassed interpersonal skills with a proven ability to quickly develop and maintain relationships with customers and colleagues.

Customer Focus
Experienced at providing a high quality service to customers at all levels, and skilled at effectively dealing with and resolving complaints.

Team Spirited
Skilled team player who adapts quickly to different team dynamics and excels at building trusting relationships with colleagues at all levels.

Employment History

Freelance Hairdresser   **Feb '03 - Present**

» Manage and maintain a customer base of over 100 clients
» Consult and advise customers
» Ensure customer satisfaction
» Provide a friendly and professional service
» Maintain up to date records and accounts

Trina's Hair Salon | Senior Stylist   **Aug '00 – Feb '03**

» Supervised and trained a team of four junior-level stylists
» Hired work experience students
» Consulted and advised customers
» Ensured customer comfort and satisfaction
» Provided a friendly and professional service

16 Any Road • Any Where
Any Town • AN8 9SE
United Kingdom

+44 (0)4587 875848
Jane.Doe@Anymail.com

Jane Doe

Continued from page 1...

My confident and
friendly nature
will enable me to
fit in and
complement
your existing team

Employment History

Trina's Hair Salon - Junior Stylist   **April '98 – Aug '00**

» Consulted and advised customers
» Ensured customer comfort and satisfaction
» Provided a friendly and professional service

Macey's Hair Salon - Receptionist   **July '96 – April '98**

» Delivered the highest level of customer service
» Ensured customer comfort
» Provided a friendly and professional service
» Assisted with enquiries and resolved complaints

Education Summary

Any College (2001)	NVQ 3 - Hairdressing
Any College (1999)	NVQ 2 - Hairdressing
Any College (1998)	NVQ 1 – Hairdressing
Any High School (1996)	11 GCSE's (grade A–D)

Certifications

British Red Cross   Basic First Aid – Sept '06

Languages

Fluent in spoken and written Spanish
Basic conversational ability in French

Activities & Interests

I have been a keen footballer for as long as I can remember and am an active member of Any Town women's football club where I have been captain of the team for 3 years. I have an active interest in nature and regularly get involved with and manage conservation assignments. To relax, I attend yoga and meditation classes that help to keep me focused and relieve stress.

16 Any Road • Any Where
Any Town • AN8 9SE
United Kingdom

+44 (0)4587 875848
Jane.Doe@Anymail.com

08:00

Prepare a Powerful Application

"Success is getting what you want. Happiness is wanting what you get"

- Dale Carnegie

Applications are primarily used to collect data from potential applicants for the purpose of evaluating their skills, qualifications, employment history and motives. Unlike résumés, which are unique to each individual, its standardised format allows selectors to quickly peruse each form and screen out any unsuitable candidates.

From the airline's perspective, the form also serves a number of other purposes. Namely: To evaluate the applicant's literacy, ability to follow instructions, penmanship and communication skills. Selection to be interviewed can be extremely competitive so recruiters will be looking or any excuse to thin the pack. A careless applicant, or one who doesn't follow instructions, will quickly disqualify themselves.

Guidance Notes

Employment History
Unless requested otherwise, your employment history should be displayed in reverse chronological order, that is starting with your most recent position and working backwards,

When describing your duties three to five action phrases have a better impact than complete sentences or generic job descriptions. Consider the following examples:

» 'As a call centre officer, I answer customer queries and complaints over the telephone'

» 'Addressed customer queries and resolved complaints'

The former example has a passive tone and is unnecessarily wordy. The latter example, on the other hand, still uses the important key words, but uses an active and punchy tone.

Most importantly, you must communicate your suitability for the position clearly by highlighting the skills and experience that are relevant and transferable. For example, a salon receptionist may include the following:

Delivered the highest level of customer service
Ensured customer comfort
Provided a friendly and professional service
Assisted with enquiries and resolved complaints

This active statement identifies customer contact experience, as well as other specific responsibilities and attributes that are required of cabin crew. It would be clear to any airline that this candidate has the necessary experience and is clearly suited for the position.

» Irrelevant positions
Where a position holds little or no relevance, short summaries are acceptable. If those positions were very brief, dated, or only part time, you may be able to safely exclude their inclusion altogether. You should only do so, however, if doing so will not create damaging gaps.

» Lack of relative experience
Most airlines will require some form of experience in a customer facing role. So if you lack experience, you should certainly get some. Whether you take on a short term voluntary post at a local charity shop or some weekend bar work, you will surely strengthen your application.

» Fragmented work history
A fragmented job history, one that is made up of lots of short-term jobs, will not present a favourable impression to a potential employer. Fortunately, there are several options you can consider which will minimise its impact:

A process of elimination
If eliminating brief, dated, irrelevant, or part time jobs will not create damaging gaps, you should consider doing so

Spring into summer
Instead of listing specific dates for summer jobs, you can simply state Summer 20xx to Spring 20xx.

Consecutive combining
Where several similar consecutive jobs appear, you can combine them into one chunk, for example:

2004–2006   Receptionist
                   Aztec Hotel & Spa, Bloomfields Leisure,
                   Trina's Hair & Beauty Salon

» Gaps in employment
If you have gaps in your employment history, you may be asked to elaborate on these. Whatever your reasons: maternity leave, study or travel break, be honest and positive, and be prepared to discuss the details openly.

If you were doing anything during the gaps, paid or unpaid, it would be ideal to insert them into your work history to fill the gaps.

For example:
2005–2009   Full Time Parent
Summer 2004–Spring 2005   Travelled around Europe

» Career progression
If you have remained with an employer for several years but have progressed through the ranks, you can make your progression more obvious by listing each position as you would a new job.

» Reasons for leaving
While your reason for leaving your current employment is probably for career advancement, you should consider expanding on this, if space permits, to make it more memorable. For example:

"To advance my career as cabin crew with an airline that I admire"

Your reasons for leaving your previous employment may be for any reason: career advancement, not enough hours, wider responsibilities, temporary contract, redundancy, maternity leave, study break, travel break, or company relocation. Whatever your reason, remain positive and avoid phrases such as fired, terminated, quit, illness and personal reasons,

If you were fired or quit under less than favourable conditions, avoid drawing attention to the fact by using neutral phrases such as 'job ended'. Alternatively, you can simply state 'Will explain at the interview'. Both of these will provide you with the opportunity to discuss the details openly at interview where you can create a more favourable and detailed response.

Remember, you should not lie about your reasons for leaving previous employment posts as they are grounds for dismissal in the future.

Leisure Interests
Recreational interests create depth and humanises your character. A targeted list, which focuses on relevant skills, will form an immediate and positive impression. They also serve as excellent sources of additional skills and experiences, which can be advantageous if you lack employment experience.

Generalised list statements such as: 'reading, watching television, sport and socialising' should be avoided, as should unprofessional statements such as: 'I enjoy spending time with my mates, hitting the town and going out on the razz".

To enhance your application form positively, focus and expand on those interests that have some relevance to the position. For instance, being captain of a football team demonstrates leadership qualities, while volunteering at a local charity indicates good people skills.

Here is an example: 'I have been a keen footballer for as long as I can remember and am an active member of Any Town women's football club where I have been captain of the team for 3 years. I have an active interest in nature, and regularly get involved with and manage conservation assignments. To relax, I attend yoga and meditation classes, which help to keep me focused and relieve stress.'

This statement gives an immediate impression of someone who is balanced and committed. Their interests highlight several admirable qualities such as team spirit and leadership, and it also details their methods of stress management. A recruitment office would form a positive impression of the candidate based on a statement such as this.

Awards
Outstanding excellence will show commitment and talent, so if you have achieved any awards through your activities, be sure to list them. Make sure the achievements are recent, though, as outdated awards may give the impression that you haven't achieved anything since.

References
Always get permission from the person(s) you state as your referee(s) and give them a copy of your application form or résumé to help them write a relevant reference that highlights your most important points.

If you don't have any work references that you can use, you should provide a character reference instead. This can be a school teacher, university lecturer or a friend in an authoritative position such as a police officer or doctor.

If you have been fired, or you resigned under less than favourable circumstances, you may want to call the employer to find out what they would say in response to reference checks. Usually, past employers will agree to use the term 'resigned' if you explain that your termination is hurting your chances of finding employment.

Faux Pas Alerts

Consider the following examples.

I CURRENTLY WORK AS A FREELANCE HAIRDRESSER AND HAVE WORKED IN CLIENT FACING ROLES FOR MORE THAN 8 YEARS. I AM LOOKING FOR A CHANGE IN MY LIFE DIRECTION AND FEEL THAT A CAREER AS CABIN CREW WILL GIVE ME THIS.	I curently work as freelance hairdresser & have worked in client facing roles fore more than 8 years. I am looking for a change in my life direction and feel that thet a career as cabin crew will give me this.

The first example is tidy and creates an positive impression of the candidate. Meanwhile, the second example is messy, full of typos and barely legible. It is clear that the candidate jumped straight in without planning. Hardly a positive first impression.

Stretching the Truth
Don't be tempted to just tell them what you think they want to hear. Exaggerations or untruths can come back to haunt you if you're are quizzed about them at the interview, or even later in employment. Be equally mindful about over indulging as the recruiter may get the impression that your hobbies will take priority over your work.

Additional Information / Personal Statement

At the end of most application forms, you will be presented with some form of additional information box. This box may simply state 'Additional Information',or it could be more specific, such as:

» Please state your reason for applying and why you feel you are suited to the position of cabin crew?

» Please provide further information which you feel will benefit your application

Essentially, this is an opportunity to sell yourself and you should use it to provide a power statement which summarises your experience, highlights your key skills, and shares your motives all within a few short paragraphs.

Consider the following example:

'As you will note, I have eight years experience within the retail industry. Within which, I have built extensive customer relations, team working and supervisory experience, which has also greatly enhanced my communication and interpersonal skills.

With these skills and experiences, combined with my passion for the airline industry, my motivation to succeed, strong attention to detail, and unparalleled work ethic, I am confident that I will make a positive contribution to the airline and excel as a member of the Fly High cabin crew team.

I would welcome the opportunity to meet with you to discuss this position and my background in more detail, and to explore the ways I could contribute to the ongoing success of your airline.'

The above example is concise. It focuses on what the candidate can offer the airline, rather than what the airline can offer the candidate, and it showcases skills and experiences that are an asset for a cabin crew position.

Fly High Airlines

Application for Cabin Crew Employment

All information supplied will be treated as confidential.
Subject to meeting the eligibility criteria, you will be invited to attend our next selection day.
Correct information will be a condition of employment.

Full Name (Mr / Mrs / Ms)   **JANE DOE**   Date Available   **29/01/11**

Present Address	**Permanent Address** (If different)
22 Any Street Any TowN ANY WHERE	N/A

Post Code	**AN2 6DG**	Country	**U.K**	Post Code	**N/A**	Country	**N/A**

Please give telephone numbers in the format: Country Code + City/Mobile Code + Phone Number

Telephone (Residence)	**44 1179 637264**	Telephone (Residence)	**N/A**
Telephone (Mobile)	**44 798 837472**	Telephone (Mobile)	**N/A**
Email	**Jane.doe@anymail.com**		

Personal Information

Passport Number:	**2048374638**	Expiry Date:	**09/2021**
Date of Birth:	**11/09/1979**	Gender:	**female**
Marital Status:	**single**	Nationality:	**british**

Height (cm)   **154**   Weight (kg)   **49**

Do you have tattoos or body piercings?   **No**   If yes, please specify   **N/A**

How would you rate your ability to swim?   **AVERAGE ABILITY unaided**

Education   *Please continue on a separate sheet if necessary*

From	To	Name & Address of School/College	Subject(s)	Results
09/99	07/01	Any college - any where - an8 7kd	hairdressing	nvq 3 - distinction
09/98	07/99	Any college - any where - an8 7kd	hairdressing	nvq 2 - merit
09/97	07/98	Any college - any where - an8 7kd	hairdressing	nvq 1 - distinction
09/91	07/96	any school - any where - an8 375	english / geography french / art / cdt maths / science / maths	8 gcse's grade a-c

Present/Last Employer

Employer:	Self employed	From:	01/02/03	To:	Present
Position:	Hairdresser	Salary:		15,000 pa	
Address:	n/a	Notice Required:		None	
		Reason for Leaving:		To pursue a career as cabin crew	

Responsibilities: Manage and maintain a customer base of over 100 clients
Consult and advise customers
Ensure customer satisfaction
Provide a friendly and professional service
Maintain up to date records and accounts

Previous Employment   *Please continue on a separate sheet if necessary*

Employer:	Trina's hair salon	From:	16/02/00	To: 01/02/03
Address:	159 Any city centre any town - an9 6dj	Responsibilities:		Supervised and trained a team of four junior-level stylists - Hired work experience students - Consulted and advised customers - Ensured customer comfort and satisfaction - Provided a friendly and professional service
Position	senior hair stylist			
Reason for Leaving:	to pursue freelance opportunity			

Employer:	Trina's hair salon	From:	05/04/98	To: 16/08/00
Address:	159 Any city centre any town - an9 6dj	Responsibilities:		Consulted and advised customers - Ensured customer comfort and satisfaction - Provided a friendly and professional service
Position	junior hair stylist			
Reason for Leaving:	to pursue promotion opportunity			

Employer:	MACEY's hair salon	From:	24/07/97	To: 05/04/98
Address:	378 Any city centre any town - an5 6sj	Responsibilities:		Delivered the highest level of customer service - Ensured customer comfort - Provided a friendly and professional service - Assisted with enquiries and resolved complaints
Position	receptionist			
Reason for Leaving:	to pursue promotion opportunity			

Please explain any gaps in unemployment

upon leaving school in 1996, i spent a year travelling before moving into employment

Please list any voluntary work

For the last three years, i have volunteered at the samaritans homeless shelter during the christmas period, where i help cook and serve beverages

Additional Training

Give details of any first aid and/or nursing qualifications

british red cross - basic first aid training - 09/2006

Give details of languages spoken and abilities

English - native language
french - read, write and speak fluently
spanish - basic conversational ability

Give details of any other training

i have attended, and passed, short courses in leadership and communication

Hobbies/Outside Interests

I have been a keen footballer for as long as I can remember and am an active member of Any Town women's football club where I have been captain of the team for 3 years. I have an active interest in nature and regularly get involved with and manage conservation assignments. To relax, I attend yoga and meditation classes that help to keep me focused and relieve stress.

Use the following space to provide any further information that you feel will benefit your application

As you will note, I have an extensive eight years experience within the retail industry. Within these roles, I have built extensive customer relations, team working and supervisory experience, and greatly enhanced my communication and interpersonal skills.

With these skills and experiences, combined with my passion for the airline industry, my motivation to succeed, strong attention to detail, and unparalleled work ethic, I am confident that I will make a positive contribution to the airline and excel as a member of the Fly High cabin crew team.

Declaration

Have you ever been convicted of a criminal offence which, at the date of application, is not a spent conviction as defined in the Rehabilitation of Offenders Act 1974? Yes/No
If yes, then such convictions must be disclosed below.

n/a

Have you ever been refused entry, or deported from a foreign country? Yes/No
If yes, please provide further details.

n/a

The details provided on this application are correct to my knowledge and belief. I understand that my application may be rejected or that I may be dismissed for withholding relevant information or giving false information. I am aware that my employment with Fly High Airlines will be subject to satisfactory references, medical form and criminal record checks.

Signature   Date   05/01/2011

Going Digital

The only significant difference between a digital application form and its paper counterpart is how they are completed. The questions will be similar and both require the same effort. Before you proceed, here are some useful pointers for you to follow:

» Be prepared
  Before you proceed with the online form, have an up to date résumé to hand so that you have relevant details in front of you for reference.

» Offline drafting
  The benefit of using a word processing package to draft and save you answers is threefold. Firstly, you will have a back up if any problems occur with the online form. Secondly, you will be able to run a spell check before you copy the information into the online system. Thirdly, your information will not be lost if your session times out (See the note below).

» Follow the instructions
  The online system should guide you through the process, so follow any instructions carefully. In most cases there will be a help button if you get really stuck.

» Keep a record
  Most online forms offer the option of storing your application for later completion or revision. If you choose to do this, be sure to keep a record of any user names and passwords so that you can sign back in.

» Time out
  Some online application forms have a time out facility, whereby the session will close after a period of inactivity. If a system such as this is in place, there will usually be a timer displayed. However, this may not always be the case so you should always save your progress.

» Submission
  Don't press the submit button until you have backed up your answers, proofread the application form and are 100% happy with your entries. Once it has been submitted, you can't reverse the submission.

Part 3

Attend

"The most important single ingredient in the formula of success is knowing how to get along with people"

- Theodore Roosevelt

09:00

The Group Assessment

"One secret of success in life is for man to be ready for his opportunity when it comes"

- Benjamin Disraeli

What to Expect

There is no set formula as to how many or which combination of activities are included during airline assessments, however, the process is typically divided into three key segments, these are: Group activities, individual assessments and a panel interview.

» Group activities
  During the group segment, you will be asked to take part in several activities. These activities are designed to reveal your personality, competencies and potential for working as cabin crew and are likely to include a series of practical tasks, group discussions and role plays.

» Individual assessments
  Individual assessments may be paper based, such as personality questionnaires and general knowledge tests, or they may be practical, such as self presentations, language proficiency and reach tests. Either way, these assessments form an integral part of the eligibility criteria.

» Panel interview
  A typical panel interview will take place before two or three recruitment officers. While each member of the panel will have an opportunity to pose questions to the candidate, it is common practice to have a primary examiner to ask questions and a secondary examiner to observe and take notes.

Attendance
The volume of attendees will depend on the airline and the assessment procedure. Typically, invitation only assessment days will accommodate fewer than 30 candidates, while open days can attract a hundred or more.

Venue
Invitation only assessments and final interviews are typically held at the airlines own premises. Open days attract a larger attendance so will commonly be held within a hotel establishment.

Schedule
The assessment process varies considerably in length and structure depending on a number of factors. In some instances, they may span only a few short hours. In other cases, they may be split over a series of days. Your invitation letter or the airlines website will provide further confirmation of the predicted schedule.

For reference, panel interviews may be as short as 20 minutes or as long as two hours.

Eliminations
During the group and individual assessments, eliminations of unsuccessful candidates will take place periodically throughout the event.

Meet the Candidates

Successful interation with your fellow candidates is essential if you are to create a good impression. This can be a daunting prospect for some, so I have devised some guidelines and strategies that will carry you through and see you shine.

Friend or foe?
Whether fellow candidates are friends or foes matters not. The recruiters will be assessing your ability to positively interact with others so it is important to be friendly, considerate and respectful to everyone you meet.

Successful interaction
Successful interaction comes from understanding and respecting an individuals' personality. Read through the following personality guidelines to learn how to effectively interact with the varying types you are likely to encounter.

» The Aggressor
The aggressors that you will encounter in an interview environment are often covert and manipulative. They disguise their attacks as constructive criticism or harmless jokes so that, in the instance that they are confronted, they can deny any wrong doing. If you find yourself under attack from these predators, ask questions that will temp them into the open, such as: "That sounded like a disrespectful comment, was it?"

If the aggressor is more openly disrespectful and disparaging, the best approach is to remain calm and composed, listen attentively and without interruption until they have finished. A counter attack will only reflect badly on you so resist the tendency to fight back. Instead, acknowledge their opinion and then voice your own in a respectful manner.

» The Extrovert
Extroverts are very sociable creatures and thrive on interaction. They are comfortable speaking to large audiences, are very open with their thoughts and feelings, and take an enthusiastic approach to most activities.

As these extroverted types love to network, any time spent in discussion with them may be somewhat limited. While in their presence, enjoy the buzz they create and allow their enthusiasm to radiate through you.

If you have an introverted tendency, there may be a potential personality clash. Just bide you time and try to enjoy their vibrant presence.

» The Desperado
Some candidates will be in a position of sheer desperation for the job. Whether this is due to a real need or a simple desire, these individuals are likely to appear anxious and tense. Be friendly and empathetic with these candidates, but avoid getting drawn too deeply into conversation about of their hardship.

» The Model
In using the term 'model', I am not necessarily referring to looks. Rather, I am referring to those candidates who seem to be models of perfection. They appear to say and do all the right things, seemingly without a care or worry in the world. They naturally exude charisma and confidence, and have a magnetic personality.

In observing these candidates, examine what makes them appear perfect and then learn by their example. How do they stand? What do they do with their hands? How do they use their voice?

» The Overly Anxious
  Some individuals become overwhelmed at interviews and will experience intense levels of stress, fear and panic. In this heightened state, the individual may experience uncontrollable symptoms such as blushing, stammering and shaking.

  Experiencing a panic attack is very traumatic, so be friendly and supportive with these individuals. Offer words of encouragement, but don't place too much focus on their anxiety. Rather, try to break their state by asking questions about things they enjoy and that make them feel relaxed. You could ask them about their family, hobbies or desires.

» The Dominator
  Can't get a word in? You may be encountering the dominator. In milder cases, dominators like to be the centre of attention and will talk incessantly to control the conversation. In extreme cases, they will be argumentative, rude and irrational.

  In the face of a domineering person, remain calm and resist the natural urge to reason or retaliate. Instead, you should either try to distance yourself from the person, otherwise an assertive communication style is needed to push past this stickler. In this instance, remain calm, confident and respectful.

» The Actor
  Actors in this context refers to those candidates who put on an elaborate front to conceal their true personalities. These individuals are usually relatively harmless so, if you do happen to catch their act, it is probably best to not blow their cover.

  If, however, it becomes obvious that this candidate has blatantly lied for the job, you may want to distance yourself to avoid being associated with their deceit.

» The Know-It-All
  Know-it-alls have an attitude of superiority and like to think they are experts in everything. In conversation, they are arrogant and condescending and openly disregard the opinion of others. Some know-it-alls really are experts, so just agree with them and try to move on. If, however, the so called expert is not an expert at all, simply state the facts as you perceive them. Whatever you do, don't be drawn into a debate with either type because it will get messy.

» The Negativist
Ah, the negativist. There's always one in every crowd. At best, negativists are very annoying. At worst, they will drain every ounce of energy and motivation from your body. Attempts to motivate or encourage these people generally fall flat, so it's sometimes best not to say anything at all. So, remain positive and try to distance yourself as much as possible. If this is not possible, detach yourself from their words and stay focused on your own positive energy.

» The Leader
Natural leaders are instantly recognisable by their innate desire to step up. Their confident, assertive and intelligent character inspires trust in others while their sensitive, inspiring and sincere side inspires confidence. In the presence of a good leader, respect, support and encourage their efforts. Participate and be an active member of their team.

» The Show-off
You can be certain to find a show-off at every cabin crew interview. You will recognise him or her by their showy, self absorbed and obnoxious attitude. While this personality type is easily annoying, the truth is that these people tend to be deeply insecure. They brag about their own achievements through fear that nobody will otherwise notice. So, be kind and sincerely acknowledge their efforts when appropriate.

» The Rival
Naturally there will be candidates present who view you as competition and a threat to their success. Being competitive isn't a bad thing in itself unless these candidates put up barriers and become inwardly focused. In this instance, it is important to be friendly while respectful of their space. Remember, competitive people are passionate, driven and innovative, so embrace these positive traits.

» The Gossiper
Some individuals like to point out other peoples flaws or failures in an attempt to feel superior. Beware of these gossiping individuals as you can be sure they will gossip about you too. In the first instance, attempt to change the subject. If they continue, discourage their behaviour directly by refusing to participate. If all fails, take your leave immediately.

» The Entertainer
Entertainers thrive on interaction. They are sociable, talkative and very energetic people and love to be the centre of attention. It is very easy to like the entertainer as they have a very down to earth and friendly attitude. When interacting with an entertainer, avoid being overly serious and just allow their positive energy to flow through you.

Meet the Recruitment Officers

Typically, there will be two or three official recruitment officers present during recruitment days. These officers may be HR personnel, or they may be working senior crew members. Either way, you can be sure that they are experienced recruitment professionals.

Successful interaction
To successfully interact with recruitment personnel, it is important to understand their styles and be prepared to deal with them accordingly. Within a cabin crew interview setting, you will typically encounter two dominant styles of interviewer. I call these: The interrogation experts and the guardian angels.

» The interrogation expert
Interrogation experts believe that candidates will only show their true personalities while under intense pressure. As a result, they adopt a direct and intimidating style of questioning and will cross examine every answer you provide. During this onslaught of questioning, they will be observing your ability to remain calm and think on your feet. So, approach their questions in a calm and confident manner and be direct and succinct in your response.

» The guardian angel
Guardian angels believe that candidates are more open and natural when they feel relaxed. Thus, they will attempt to relieve the pressure of the atmosphere by engaging in friendly conversation. While their relaxed and friendly style can be a welcome relief, unsuspecting candidates may become overly casual and reveal more than is appropriate. Thus, caution is advised. The key is to be friendly yet professional, and never let your guard down.

Meet the Undercover Team

To help the recruitment officers make informed decisions and better elimination choices, undercover officers are often placed among the group during recruitment days. Within the role of a fellow candidate, these officers can observe individuals in their relaxed and natural state and be in a better position to identify unsuitable candidates.

These officers are largely accountable for the high percentage of failure rates that candidates experience during the group stage. They are also the reason why some candidates leave the interview feeling confused about their elimination.

Unfortunately, these officers are very good at their jobs, so there is little chance that you will ever identify them. However, simply being aware of their presence will give you a great advantage as you will be able to adapt your strategy to avoid this devastating outcome.

Impress
To impress undercover officers, you simply need to treat everyone you meet in the same positive manner. If you are friendly, respectful and supportive towards your fellow candidates, have a positive outlook and are able to demonstrate an enthusiastic attitude towards any activities which you are asked to undertake, the officers will naturally pick up on your positive energy.

The tests
To really get to the bare bones of a candidates personality, some undercover officers will conduct a series of mini personality tests. During these tests, the officer will demonstrate certain traits and then observe your reactions to them. For instance: Do you actively participate in mindless gossip, or do you show disapproval? Are you sympathetic and encouraging towards anxious candidates, or are you unsupportive and dismissive? Are you constructive in your criticism, or do you attack others ideas?

As long as you discourage others bad behaviour and actively demonstrate a positive attitude, these tests will not pose any threat to your success. In the worst instance, remain neutral until you can safely distance yourself.

10:00

Activities

> "Eighty percent of success is showing up"
>
> **- Woody Allen**

What Assessors Look For

Through your involvement and behaviour, assessors will be looking for evidence of key competencies and personality attributes that will enable you to work effectively as cabin crew and cope with the demands of the job.

The six key competencies that will be assessed are:

- » Communication skills
- » Team spirit
- » Interpersonal ability
- » Leadership
- » Customer focus
- » Initiative

To determine these competencies, the assessors will be observing:

- » Level of participation and interaction
- » Behaviour towards the activities and your peers
- » Communication and work style
- » Ability to think on your feet and react to external pressure
- » Ability to lead and willingness to follow

To make an effective evaluation, the recruiters will typically refer to a competency rating scale. This scale works on a points based system and the final result will reflect a candidates suitability for the position.

Stand out with the Seven Heavenly Virtues

1. Have fun
   However silly or irrelevant the tasks may seem, your active involvement is essential. So, rather than concern yourself about external details, just relax and allow yourself to enjoy the process. This positive viewpoint will reflect well on your character, demonstrate enthusiasm, and make the experience a fun filled one for you.

2. Contribute
   Volunteering, contributing ideas and making suggestions is another great way to demonstrate your enthusiasm and team spirit. Furthermore, it will show that you are not afraid to take the initiative or express yourself and are keen to get involved.

3. Keep track of time
   If the recruiters set a time limit for any task, it is respectful to honour the deadline. Moreover, it will reflect positively on your listening skills, and demonstrate your attention to detail and ability to follow instructions. So, remain vigilant of the time and forewarn your peers when the deadline is approaching.

4. Summarise
   Summarising the main points of a discussion is a great way to move past awkward moments of silence and sticking points. The breathing room summarising creates will typically stimulate further ideas and encourage participation. Not only will your peers be grateful for the momentary relief, your communication and leadership ability will also be highlighted.

5. Use names
   Remembering people's names will demonstrate your ability to listen and pay attention to detail. Moreover, it will demonstrate a tremendous amount of respect for others and create a lasting impact.

6. Be positive
   When you choose to exhibit a positive spirit, people will naturally be drawn towards your character. So, be enthusiastic about the exercises you are asked to undertake and be encouraging towards others.

7. Encourage
   If any members of your team remain reserved, encourage their involvement by asking if they have an idea, suggestion or opinion. This shows empathy, consideration team spirit.

Avoid the Seven Deadly Sins

1. Over involvement
   Getting involved and showing enthusiasm in a task is fantastic, but over involvement and incessant talking can leave others struggling to get involved and may transfer across to assessors as arrogance.

2. Under involvement
   For assessors to make an informed assessment, active involvement from each individual is essential. Those who are unable to get involved, for whatever reason, will surely be eliminated.

3. Disputing
   Conflicting views are natural, however, a group assessment is neither the time or place to engage in a hostile dispute with other candidates.

4. Criticising
   Even if your intentions are honourable and the feedback is constructive, criticising another candidates opinions, actions and ideas may be perceived as an attack.

5. Being negative
   Making negative remarks or exhibiting frustration over tasks, peers or previous employers , no matter how harmless it may seem, will raise serious concerns about your attitude and ethics.

6. Being bossy
   There is nothing wrong with striving for excellence, however, being dominant and imposing your ideas on others is overbearing and intimidating which leads others to feel incompetent.

7. Neglecting to listen
   Neglecting to listen to instructions leads to misinterpretations and displays a general lack of enthusiasm. Not listening or talking over others is ignorant and disrespectful.

Common Concerns

Being alienated
When there are a lot of different personalities in a group and the emotions are high, it can become difficult to get involved. This is especially true during a large group discussion. In these instances, you should employ some of the following strategies for getting your voice heard.

» Raise your hand
As simple as it seems, raising your hand will demand the attention of the group and let them know that you have something to say.

» Be assertive
If raising your hand reaps no results, you will have to be more assertive. Wait for a momentary pause in the conversation, and simple say "excuse me" before proceeding. This may feel uncomfortable for some of you, but it is imperative that you contribute. If done calmly and respectfully, the assessors will be impressed by your effort.

Dealing with anxiety

If you have read through and practised the techniques described in the previous section, you should not experience much difficulty in dealing with symptoms of anxiety.

For on the spot relief, the most effective techniques are:

» Subtle deep breathing

» Trigger positive anchors

» Silently repeat affirmations

» Change your focus

Whichever technique you use, don't allow it to distract your attention too much that you lose the flow of the discussion or task.

Handling disagreements

If you disagree with an approach being taken by the group or an idea which has been brought forth, it is perfectly reasonable to say so as long as you are constructive and positive in doing so.

Consider the following statements:

» Negative:
"That wouldn't work. I think we should…"

» Constructive:
"I see your point, Mark, but there are a number of issues that may arise with that approach. How about we consider…"

The former example attacks and ridicules the idea, while the latter demonstrates a positive acknowledgement before a new idea is introduced.

In the instance that your new idea is rejected, remain polite and seek input from the group. If you are clearly outnumbered, gracefully accept the decision and move on.

Being ridiculed
If your idea is ridiculed, resist the temptation to retaliate. Instead, remain cordial and respectful in your response. This graceful reaction will be duly noted and respected by the assessors.

Feeling uncertain
You don't always have to give an opinion when you speak. Supporting what someone else has said, asking a legitimate question, or commenting on an emerging theme are equally good ways to make your presence known without appearing as if you like the sound of your own voice.

Points to Consider

In most cases, the outcome of each task or topic is largely irrelevant. Assessors are more concerned with how well you perform in a team environment, how you communicate your ideas and interact with others, and what role you typically assume.

Thus, no matter how you feel, you should approach every task with a can do attitude and every topic in a calm and conversational tone.

11:00

Practical Tasks

"Success is simple. Do what's right, the right way, at the right time"

- Arnold H. Glasow

Bridging the Gap

Instructions

With the materials provided, design and construct a bridge which strong enough to support a roll of sticky tape.

Materials

- » 5 sheets of A4 paper
- » A pair of scissors
- » 1 Metre length of sticky tape
- » 4 Drinking straws
- » 1 Metre length of string
- » 2 Elastic bands

Bridging the Gap

Instructions

With the materials provided, design and construct a bridge which strong enough to support a roll of sticky tape.

Materials

- » 5 sheets of A4 paper
- » A pair of scissors
- » 1 Metre length of sticky tape
- » 4 Drinking straws
- » 1 Metre length of string
- » 2 Elastic bands

Advertising Space

Instructions

Fly High Airlines has secured a prime time radio spot and needs a new commercial campaign.

Using the teams collective knowledge of the airline, create a compelling commercial that will attract new customers.

The final broadcast must be no more than 45 seconds in length, and each team member must have an active role in the final presentation.

Points to Consider

This activity will highlight your knowledge of the airline, so be ready with plenty of input from your research.

Attention Please

Instructions

Many passengers ignore safety demonstrations because they feel they have heard it all before.

In an effort to increase safety, Fly High Airlines is considering an overhaul of its safety procedures.

As a group, come up with a safety demonstration which will encourage passengers to pay attention to these important briefings.

The demonstration can include appropriate humour, choreography and melodies, but the outcome should be no more than five minutes in length.

Let Me Entertain You

Instructions

As you reach cruising altitude, you discover that the in flight entertainment system has failed. To ensure the passengers are entertained for the duration of the four hour flight, design a game concept and present it to the rest of the group in a teaching style.

Who's Who?

Instructions

Pair off with a random partner and try to find out as much as you can about each other in twenty minutes.

When called upon, present your partner to the group.

Points to Consider

The purpose of this task is threefold.:

- » How relevant is the information you gather?
- » How confident are you when addressing a group?
- » How well do you interact with new people.

Designer Wear

Instructions

Fly High Airlines is looking to update its image and needs new designs for its cabin crew uniform.

Consider the existing design and come up with a new or modified concept.

Points to Consider

During this task, be mindful of what is considered appropriate to the culture.

Also, take inspiration from the current design as it provides valuable insight into what the airline considers to be appropriate.

12:00

Discussions

"Failure is not an option. Everyone has to succeed"

- Arnold Schwarzenegger

Shipwrecked

Instructions

The plane has gone down over the Atlantic Ocean. There are eight survivors, but the one surviving life raft only has a capacity for four people.

As a team, identify four survivors from the following list who you would save and why. Select a spokes-person to present your decision and explain why you came up with the results.

Survivors

- » The pilot
- » A pregnant woman
- » An ex army general
- » A surgeon
- » The pope
- » A child
- » A nurse
- » An athlete

Points to Consider

Due to the very nature of this task, there is a potential for some strong emotions to be released. In such instances, remain calm and don't be tempted into a confrontation. Simply acknowledge and show respect for others opinions.

Survivor

Instructions

Your flight is scheduled to land in Los Angeles, however, due to mechanical difficulties the plane was forced to land on a remote island.

During landing, much of the equipment aboard was damaged, but 10 items have been recovered intact. Your task is to rank them in terms of their importance for your crew.

Items

- » A box of matches
- » 15 feet of nylon rope
- » 5 gallons of water
- » Signal flares
- » A self inflating life raft

- » A magnetic compass
- » First aid kit
- » A fruit basket
- » A tub of dry milk powder
- » A shotgun

Rags to Riches

Instructions

You have just won £1,000,000.00 on the lottery. From the five options below, which action would you take and why?

Options

- » Take early retirement
- » Give a large percentage to charity
- » Invest it into a business
- » Save it for your future
- » Spend it on luxuries

Day Trip

Instructions

You have been given the responsibility for arranging a day trip for 15 disabled children. Discuss where you would take the children, what activities you would have arranged and why.

Options

» Theme park

» Museum

» White water rafting

» Trip on the Orient Express

» Water Park

» Safari

» Art gallery

» Scenic helicopter ride

Points to Consider

In this instance, the children in question are disabled. So, certain activities will not be appropriate, while others may not sufficiently capture the children's interest. It is important to gain a balance between having fun and being safe.

13:00

Role Plays

> "The starting point of achievement, is desire"
>
> **- Napoleon Hill**

Role play scenarios may be performed with other candidates as a pair or within a group, or they may be performed one on one with an assessor.

The scenarios will bear some relation to the demands of the job and are likely to include:

- » Intoxicated passenger
- » Disorderly behaviour
- » Terrorist threat
- » Disruptive child

- » Toilet smoker
- » Abusive behaviour
- » Fearful passenger
- » Passenger complaint

The assessors don't expect you to know the answer to every possible scenario they introduce. They simply want to see how you react in challenging situations. So, when taking part in any role play scenario, use the following guidelines:

- » Be proactive and do your best to resolve the situation using your initiative
- » Remain calm and composed

» Be direct and assertive

» Immerse yourself into the role

» Take each scenario seriously

» Devise a plan and follow it as much as possible

Here are some pointers to help you deal with some common scenarios:

» Complaint
In the case of a passenger complaint, it is important that you listen to their concern without interruption. Ask questions, where appropriate, to clarify their concerns and show empathy towards their situation. If the facts warrant it, apologise for the situation, explain what action you intend to take and thank them for bringing the matter to your attention.

» Fearful passenger
If a passenger is fearful of flying, be considerate of their feelings. Use a gentle and calm tone to talk them through the flight and reassure them of any sounds or sensations they may experience. Let the passenger know where you can be found and show them the call bell.

» Intoxicated passenger
Offer the passenger a cup of tea or coffee and don't provide any more alcoholic drinks. You could also encourage the passenger to eat some food. Remain calm towards the passenger, but be direct and assertive in your approach. If you feel it appropriate, inform your senior and seek assistance from other crew members.

14:00

Individual Assessments

> "Every problem is a gift - without problems we would not grow"
>
> **- Anthony Robbins**

What to expect

Individual assessments usually involve a mix of paper based questionnaires and verbal presentations. These assessments are very basic in nature and involve only a general level of proficiency.

The assessments each airline conducts will represent what they consider to be most important. For example, some airlines, such as Virgin Atlantic, may require above average presentation skills and will, therefore, require candidates to carry out a self presentation. Another airline, such as Emirates, may not assess this ability at all.

With a little prior prepartion, these assessments shouldn't prove to be a problem and you'll be able to pass them with ease.

15:00

Self Introduction

> "You cannot control what happens to you, but you can control your attitude toward what happens to you, and in that, you will be mastering change rather than allowing it to master you"

- Brian Tracy

As well as learning more about you and your background, the self introduction is an opportunity for the recruiters to assess how well you cope when addressing a group of people and how articulately you are able to communicate your message. In their assessment, they will be looking for good delivery, and a certain amount of charisma.

To deliver a self introduction which makes an impact, here are some guidelines for you to consider.

» Make it relevant
  Use this opportunity to highlight your suitability for the job of cabin crew by sharing interesting facts about your present or most recent job, and your motives for making a career change.

  Consider the following example:
  " Hi everyone. My name is Jane and it's really nice to meet you all. I'm 27 years old and live in the bustling city of Bristol. I currently work as a freelance hair consultant, which is a job I really enjoy, but I have always wanted to be cabin crew which is why I am here today. Outside of work, I enjoy horse riding and am captain of the local football team"

» Be spontaneous
  A self presentation which is spontaneous will add life and sincerity to your speech. Sure you can prepare a rough draft and familiarise yourself with it, but don't try to learn it by heart as there is a risk of appearing forced, dull and monotone.

» Inject personality
  Show your passion and enthusiasm by injecting some emotion into your presentation.

» Be concise
  Unless advised otherwise, keep it relatively short and focused. Thirty to Sixty seconds should be sufficient.

» Rotate your focus
  To give the impression of confidence and engage your audience, rotate your gaze and make eye contact with various members for three to five seconds each.

» Adjust your voice
  Varying your tone, pitch, volume and pace will eliminate monotone and make it enjoyable for others to listen to. Slowing your pace slightly will also add clarity.

» Stick to the time limit
  If a time limit has been set, be sure to respect it.

16:00

Personality Questionnaire

"Focus on where you want to go, not on what you fear"

- Anthony Robbins

Through a series of simple questions, personality tests provide assessors with an indication of a candidates character, behaviour and work style. The test results merely supplement the recruiters own observations from the interview and, as such, there are no right or wrong answers.

Typical questions you will encounter are:

For each question, give a mark out of five. One = Disagree strongly | Five = Agree strongly	
» I enjoy meeting new people.	
» I get bored with repetitive tasks.	
» I often lose my temper when I am frustrated.	
» I always think before I act.	
» I work well under pressure.	
» I find it easy to relax.	
» I get on well with most people.	
» I am a team player.	
» I prefer to work alone.	
» I become nervous in social situations.	
» I find it difficult to communicate with other cultures.	
» I thrive on challenges.	

In an attempt to create a favourable impression, some candidates try to imagine how the recruiters want them to be and will answer questions dishonestly. I would advise against this strategy because any contradiction between your answers and the recruiters own observations will make it obvious that the answers have been embellished.

Tips for Success

When completing any kind of written test, it is important that you read the questions through fully and make sure you completely understand what is being asked before attempting to answer.

To be confident that you have answered as many questions as possible, it is always best to complete the questions you find easy on the first pass, returning to the trickier questions later.

To avoid handing in a form that is full of scribbles and mistakes, mark your answers out in pencil and carry out a final proof-read before you hand in your form.

17:00

Language Proficiency Test

"Move out of your comfort zone. You can only grow if you are willing to feel awkward and uncomfortable when you try something new."

- Brian Tracy

If a second language is a requirement of the airline or if English isn't your native language, you may be required to complete a language assessment based on the following four key skills:

» Listening

» Reading

» Writing

» Speaking

Performance will be evaluated by how well the candidate understands and can be understood.

Listening
In this section of the test, you will have the chance to show how well you understand the spoken language.

Questions you may come across are as follows:

» You will see a picture, and you will hear four short statements. When you hear the statements, look at the picture and choose the statement that best describes what you see in the picture.

» You will hear a question or statement, followed by three responses. You are to choose the best response to each question or statement.

» You will hear a short conversation between two people. You will then read a question about each conversation. The question will be followed by four answers. You are to choose the best answer to each question.

Reading

In this section of the test, you will have the chance to show how well you understand the written language.

Here are some examples:

Choose one word which best completes the following sentence.

Because the equipment is very delicate, it must be handled with _____.

(A) Caring   (B) Careful   (C) Care   (D) Carefully

Identify one underlined word which should be corrected or rewritten.

All employees are repaired to wear their identification badges while at work.

(A) employees   (B) repaired   (C) wear   (D) identification

Writing & Speaking

In the written and spoken sections of the test, you will have the chance to show how well you speak and write the language.

You may be asked basic questions about your home town, family, work or study, leisure and future plans.

18:00

Numerical Ability Test

. . . .

"It is the way we react to circumstances that
determines our feelings."

- Dale Carnegie

Numeracy tests are designed to test your basic arithmetic skills: Addition, subtraction, multiplication and division. While they are typically short and relatively simple in nature, if you haven't exercised your maths brain for some time, it may be a good idea to practice some basic mental arithmetic before the interview.

Here are some sample questions to get your juices flowing.

Calculators may or may not be permitted.

1. What is Twelve Thousand Nine Hundred and Seventy Six in figures?
A. 129,76.00   B. 12,976,000   C. 12,976.00

2. What is 6 multiplied by 8?
A. 48   B. 52   C. 46

3. Add 67 to 12
A. 80   B. 79   C. 76

4. You begin with a float of 66.94. A customer purchases a pack of peanuts at 0.66, a shot of spirits at 3.54 and a pack of chewing gum at 0.53. How much float should you have following this transaction?
A. 62.21   B. 71.76   C. 71.67

5. There are 357 seats on your aircraft. The seats are divided into three cabins. How many seats are in each cabin?

A. 117   B. 119   C. 109

Tips for Success

» Run through your times tables

» Practice some basic calculations like subtraction and multiplication

» Practice estimating answers without the use of a calculator

» Read each question and answer carefully - sometimes multiple choice answers are deliberately similar so take time to check each option. Pay particular attention to things like the unit of measurement or the number of decimal places.

19:00

Miscellaneous Tests

""It doesn't matter where you are coming from. All that matters is where you are going."

- Brian Tracy

Reach Test

Where an airline doesn't have a minimum height requirement, they may have a reach requirement instead. A reach requirement simply requires the ability to reach necessary components inside the aircraft which are typically between 6' (182 cm) and 6'10" (212 cm).

To determine candidates reach ability, a simple reach test may be conducted whereby a mark is placed on the wall, typically 6'10" from the floor, and the candidate is asked to reach for the line from their bare feet.

General Knowledge Quiz

General knowledge tests are fairly straightforward. The questions cover a broad range of topics and are likely to include political, geographical, historical, entertainment and scientific areas.
Here are some sample test questions to give you a better idea of what to expect.

- » In relation to time, what does the abbreviation GMT stand for?
- » How many continents are there?
- » What is the name of the highest mountain in the world?

- » Which is the largest continent?
- » What is the capital of the USA?
- » In which country would you find the river Nile?
- » In which continent would you find Russia?
- » Who is the president of the United States?
- » Where will the next Olympics be held?

Medical Questionnaire

The preemployment medical questionnaire is a simple form which asks you to confirm your current level of medical health and declare any history of serious illness, or drug and alcohol abuse.

Affirming certain conditions isn't an automatic failure of your application, so complete the form as accurately as possible. If you have had a condition which has been treated or is being successfully controlled, clearly state this.

Don't lie or leave out important information as it will be evident when the full medical examination is carried out by the airline.

20:00

Prepare for the Panel

"If you are not in the process of becoming the person you want to be, you are automatically engaged in becoming the person you don't want to be"

- Dale Carnegie

What Assessors Look For

Having assessed your involvement during the group session, the recruiters will now seek to explore your motives for applying to their airline and your desire for pursuing a career as cabin crew. Moreover, they will seek to gather information about your work history, character and work ethic to determine whether you will fit the job and airline.

During the interview, they will examine your ability to listen actively, express yourself articulately, confidently and professionally, and answer questions logically and concisely. They will also be paying special attention to how you present yourself.

The Process

To ease you into the interview process and make you feel more open and relaxed, the recruiters will typically open the session with questions about you and your background.

They will then seek to explore your motivation for applying to the airline and making a career change. Questions such as "Why do you want to work for us?" and "Why do you want to be cabin crew?" are common at this stage.

With the interview thoroughly under way, the recruiters will want to determine whether you possess the skills and experience necessary for the position. Here you can expect more probing situational and behavioural questions, such as "When have you provided good customer service?" and "Describe a time when you failed to communicate effectively".

Duration
There appears to be no typical duration for panel interviews. Some of you will be in and out in as little as 20 minutes, while others may find the interview lasts for up to two hours.

Seven Heavenly Virtues

1. Stay focused
   If you fail to control your internal dialogue you will not only lose your composure, but you also risk misunderstanding the question. Remain completely focused on what the recruiter is saying and focus on giving the best possible answer. Concerns about how you look and the outcome should be postponed until after the interview.

2. Listen actively
   Although you should never interrupt the recruiter, you shouldn't listen in total silence either. Instead, use verbal feedback cues to indicate that you are listening and that you understand. This will encourage the recruiter to continue.

   Some verbal feedback signals include: "I see", "Yes", "I understand", "Sure".

3. Inject personality
   Injecting passion and personality into your answers will add life and sincerity. It will also keep the recruiters interested in what you are saying.

4. Be concise
   If an answer is too long-winded, the recruiter will become complacent. Keeping your answers short and concise will retain their attention.

5. Be positive
   A positive spirit will reflect well on your character and allow the recruiters to warm towards you. So, be enthusiastic about the interview and the job, and speak respectfully about your previous employers and positions.

6. Vary your voice
Varying your tone, pitch, volume and pace will eliminate monotone and make it enjoyable for the recruiters to listen to. Slowing your pace slightly will also add clarity.

7. Maintain eye contact
Regular, strong eye contact will give the impression of someone who is honest and confident.

Where there is more than one recruitment officer, you should maintain eye contact with the person who asks you the question while occasionally engaging eye contact with the second recruiter.

Seven Deadly Sins

1. Controlling
Trying to lead or control the conversation will appear arrogant and disrespectful. Ask questions when appropriate opportunities arise, but allow the recruiter to do his or her job.

2. Interrupting
Interruptions are rude and disrespectful to the speaker. So, unless absolutely necessary, you should allow the recruiter to finish speaking before responding or asking for clarification.

3. Lying
If you lie, there will be a very good chance that you will be caught out when the recruiters probe into your answers with follow up questions. If this happens, you could end up looking rather silly and, worse still, any chance of being offered the job will be ruined.

4. Being negative
Making negative remarks or exhibiting frustration over tasks, peers, other airlines or previous employers, no matter how harmless it may seem, will raise serious concerns about your attitude and ethics.

5. Unprepared or unnecessary questions
To stand out as an informed and competent applicant, your questions should reflect that you have researched the airline and the position. Asking questions that have already been addressed within the airline's literature will make you appear unprepared and incompetent.

Likewise, asking questions that are based on money and benefits will make you appear selfishly motivated and give a negative impression about your motives for the position and/or the airline.

6. Talking incessantly

It's easy to talk too much when nervous, however, it is important to remember that interviews are two-way exchanges. A moment of silence, while it might seem awkward to you, lets the recruiter know that you are done and allows them to move the interview along.

7. Overusing filler words

The useless and annoying verbal mannerisms "you know," "like," "in other words," "kind of," "ummm," and "anyways." should be avoided at all costs. Besides making you sound unprofessional, they also detract attention from your message.

21:00

Competency Questions

> "Knowledge isn't power until it is applied"
>
> **- Dale Carnegie**

Preparing Examples

The key to preparing for competency-based questions is to study the job description and person specification. With this information, you can identify the core competencies that are required and prepare examples that demonstrate those competencies.

Airlines recruiting for flight attendant positions will certainly be looking for candidates who demonstrate:

- » Communication competence
- » Interpersonal ability
- » Customer focus
- » Team spirit
- » Leadership
- » Initiative

When preparing your examples, don't overlook those of a difficult or negative nature as you will surely be asked to illustrate some of these. To say that you haven't faced any difficulties would sound dishonest and naive.

Before you plunge in, however, you need to be very selective in your choices. For instance, it would be unwise to volunteer a negative example that involves a core skill, or one which had an undesirable impact on the company, colleagues or customers.

The most effective answer in this instance is one that shows that you understand that mistakes are occasionally part of the professional growth process, and that you are able to remain calm and learn from these experiences.

The S.A.R.R Formula

S.A.R.R is an acronym for Situation - Action - Result - Reflection

When preparing your examples, the S.A.R.R formula can help you structure your response.

» Situation
Begin by briefly describing the challenge, problem, or task.

» Action
Go on to describe what you did, how and why you did it.

» Result
Describe the outcome and how your actions affected the outcome or the people involved

» Reflection
Finally, you may offer a reflection. This can include what you learned from the experience and whether you would do anything differently in the future.

Consider the following example:

» Situation:
"I was in the staff room during my lunch break, and I could hear a lot of noise coming from inside the salon. I went to investigate and I was confronted by two, very bored, little girls. I could sense that their excitement was causing a disruption and inconvenience"

» Action:
"I immediately took the initiative and attempted to occupy them by offering to plait their hair while they made bracelets from some hair beads. Their eyes sparkled with excitement and I was able to keep them occupied for the remainder of their visit"

» Result:
"We had lots of fun and, while the calm was restored, the stylist was able to complete the clients' treatment"

» Reflection:
"I felt really pleased that with just a little extra effort, I had made such a big difference"

Follow up Questions

Although the S.A.R.R formula will eliminate the recruiters need to ask some follow up questions, there will always be areas that the recruiter wants to probe further into. So, it is important to have examples ready to back up any statements made.

Prepare to be asked:

» What did you learn from the experience?

» What specifically did you say?

» How did you feel?

» Would you do anything differently?

» How did they react?

» What other options did you consider?

» Why did you decide to take the action that you did?

» You mentioned ... Tell me more about that.

» How did you retain your composure?

» Can you give me an example of that?

» Can you be more specific about ...?

In some circumstances, the recruiter may even interrupt your responses with supplementary questions. Take a look at the following example.

» Candidate
"Working in a creative environment with other highly skilled professionals, it was natural that we had the occasional clash of ideas."

» Recruiter
"Please can you elaborate further?"

» Candidate
"We would sometimes have a clash of ideas based around our individual preference towards certain products, styles, magazines or equipment. Although, any disagreements we did have were relatively minor and insignificant."

» Recruiter
"What would you consider minor and insignificant?"

- » Candidate
  "Our debates were never confrontational, and they never interfered with our work in any way. In fact, some disagreements were quite educational."

- » Recruiter
  "Educational?"

- » Candidate
  "Yes, some very interesting views emerged from these debates which sometimes resulted in people, including myself, having a slight change in perspective."

- » Recruiter
  "Can you tell me about a change you had in perspective following such a debate?"

Lack of relative experience

If you don't have any relative experience in a particular area, you need to be honest and say so, but don't just leave it there. Use the opportunity to remind the recruiters of the skills that you do have or explain how you would handle the situation if it arose.

If you have faced a similar situation, you could say "I can't remember ever being in that situation, however, I did face something slightly similar that I could tell you about?".

Example Questions & Answers

When have you solved a customer problem?

The recruiter wants to get an idea of how you apply your initiative and problem-solving skills to customer related issues. A good answer here will demonstrate that you always put in extra effort to provide good customer service and are not intimidated by difficult situations.

Situation:
I remember a client who came to me to have her hair extensions replaced. She had worn sewn in extensions for several months and was experiencing some discomfort from the attachments.

Action:
As I examined her hair, I was shocked to discover how much damage had been caused. Her roots had become severely matted and the tightness from the installed tracks had created spots of baldness.

I took a moment to analyse the situation, work out a strategy and then I set to work.

I spent several hours meticulously untangling every hair and removing every extension piece, The more I removed, the more I could see the scale of the damage that had been caused. Sadly, the client's hair was in very bad shape after the removal and the spots of baldness were very evident. Needless to say, I had a very emotional customer.

I applied a very deep conditioning protein treatment to the customers remaining locks and gave it a good trim. I then finished up with some fine and strategically placed fusion hair extensions to conceal the bald patches and create some much needed volume.

Result:
Following the treatment, the client looked fantastic and her smile was restored. Her hair soon returned to its former glory and she became a regular client of mine.

When have you been confonted by an aggressive customer?

The ability to remain well-mannered and well-tempered while dealing with an aggressive customer is an absolute necessity. The recruiter will want to assess whether you can deal with confrontational issues in a calm and rational manner.

You will be assessed on how well you coped under the pressure and how you dealt with the customer. A good response will show that you never lost your temper and remained courteous throughout the experience.

Situation:
Shortly after I began freelancing, I encountered a problem when an associate of mine tried to pressure me into a free service based on friendship.

Action:
I proceeded to offer her, what I considered to be, a reasonable discount, but she was not satisfied with my offer and proceeded to pressure me with emotional blackmail. I remained cordial, but became more assertive as I continued to refuse her demands.

Result:
Rather than accept the reasons for my decision, she became increasingly enraged, and even began to slander my service and friendship

Shocked at her over-reaction, and concerned about what might develop, I felt I had no option but to withdraw from the situation.

Reflection:
This experience was very challenging and certainly tested my patience. But I remained calm and, although this particular relationship never recovered, it was a learning experience that hasn't since been repeated.

When have you had to say no to a customer?

There will be occasions when it is necessary to say no to a passenger. The recruiter wants to know that you aren't intimidated by such situations and have the strength of character to deal with the situation authoritatively, yet diplomatically.

You will be assessed on how you approached the customer and went about dealing with the situation. A good response will demonstrate your ability to use tact, and will show that you remained courteous throughout the experience.

Situation:
I remember when a customer tried to return a pair of trainers to the store for a refund. Although the customer denied it, I could see that the shoes had clearly been worn.

Action:
I remained calm and polite as I suggested that the shoes could not be returned unless faulty or unused.

The customer become very aggressive and repeatedly threatened to contact our head office to complain about me if I didn't refund him immediately.

I remained assertive and suggested this would be the best course of action for him to take. I then proceeded to provide him with the full details of our complaints manager within the head office.

Result:
Realising defeat, the man stormed out of the shop and, to my knowledge, never did take the matter further.

When have your communication skills made a difference to a situation or outcome?

The ability to communicate well is vital to the role of cabin crew, so you should have plenty of real life examples ready to share. This is your chance to shine, so don't be modest.

Situation:
I remember a trainee apprentice we had in our department who never asked questions and refused all offers of help. Unfortunately, instead of trying to understand her reasons, everyone drew the conclusion that she was a know-it-all and vowed not to offer help in the future.

Action:
Concerned that her progress would suffer, I decided to offer my encouragement and support. It soon became evident from our conversation that she had excessively high expectations of herself and feared looking incompetent. I explained that it was okay to ask questions, and mistakes were expected. I even shared a few of my own early mishaps to lighten the mood.

Result:
Very quickly after that we saw a change in her behaviour. She began asking questions, she was more open to suggestions, and her skills improved immensely.

Reflection:
From this experience, I learnt that things are not always what they appear and we need to be more objective before making rash judgements.

Tell me about a time when you struggled to fit in

With the constant rotation of crew, there will be some people that you don't immediately hit it off with. The recruiters want to know that you aren't intimidated by such difficulties and are able to move past any struggles.

Situation:
When I started working at Trina's Hair & Beauty, I was joining a very close-knit team who had been together for a number of years.

As a result of the number of trainees they had witnessed come and go over the years, they had become a little reluctant to accept new trainees.

I wouldn't say it was a struggle to fit in as such, but I certainly experienced some growing pains. With remarks such as 'if you are still here then' to contend with, I knew I had to prove myself.

Action:
To show that I was serious about the job, and was not a fly-by-night, I focused a lot of effort on learning my new job. At the same time, I continued to be friendly and respectful of my new colleagues while I made a conscious effort to get to know them.

Result:
As a result of my hard effort, It didn't take long for them to accept me and include me as part of their team. Naturally, I have become closer to some of my colleagues than with others, but we all got on and worked well as a team.

Tell me about a problem you encountered that didn't work out

No matter how hard we try, there are some instances where a problem just doesn't work out. To say otherwise will not sound honest or credible.

In answering this question, you need to first ensure that the problem was a minor one which had no negative or lasting impact on the company, a colleague or a customer. Try to accentuate the positives and keep your answer specific. Itemize the steps you took to deal with the problem and make it clear that you learnt from the experience.

Situation:
Shortly after I began freelancing, my bank returned a client's cheque to me through lack of funds.

Action:
At first, I was sure it was a mistake caused through an oversight on the part of my client. I made a number of calls, left several messages and even attempted a visit to the clients home, all to no avail.

Several weeks passed and it was clear that I was chasing a lost cause. At this point, I had to decide whether to write off the debt and blacklist the client or visit the Citizens' Advice for advice on retrieving the funds.

Result:
After careful consideration of all the factors involved, I decided to write the debt off as a learning experience.

Reflection:
In hindsight, I realise it was a silly mistake that could easily have been avoided. I have never repeated this error since as I now wait for the funds to clear before carrying out a service.

When have you made a bad decision?

We all make decisions that we regret, and to say otherwise will not sound honest or credible.

The recruiter will be assessing whether you have the character to admit and take responsibility for your mistake, whether your decision had a negative impact on customers or the company, and whether you learnt from this mistake?

In answering this question, you need to first ensure that the mistake was a minor one, which had no negative or lasting impact on the company, a colleague or a customer. Try to accentuate the positives and keep your answer specific. Itemize what you did and how you did it. Finally, you need to make it clear that you leant from the mistake and will be certain not to repeat it.

Situation:
Early in my freelance career, I was approached by a salesman who was promoting a protein conditioning system. He described the system as "The newest technology to emerge from years of research. Guaranteed to help heal, strengthen, and protect".

Although I was excited by the concept, I did have my concerns that the system sounded too good to be true. However, the salesman had all the official paperwork to back up his claims, and the literature was thorough and well presented. All these things, combined with the company's full money-back guarantee, made it appear to be a win-win situation, and a risk worth taking. So I invested.

Following my investment, I decided to test the system out on training heads before taking the system public. Unfortunately, several months of using the system passed with no obvious benefits.

Action:
Disappointed with the product, I decided to pursue the full money back guarantee, but the sales number was not recognised, and my letters were returned unopened. Even their website had mysteriously vanished. I soon came to the realisation that I had been taken in by an elaborate scam.

I contacted the Citizens Advice Bureau and Trading Standards, but there was little they could do to retrieve my funds.

Result:
Unfortunately, I never recovered my costs and had to put the mistake down to a learning experience.

Reflection:
Unfortunately, it really was my fault. I should have trusted my gut instinct and carried out thorough research before making my decision. It is a mistake I shall never repeat.

22:00

Traditional Questions

> "If you're passionate about what it is you do, then you're going to be looking for everything you can to get better at it"

- Jack Canfield

Why do you want to become cabin crew?

An honest and passionate response to this question will surely set you apart. Think about it, why do you really want the job? Where did the desire come from? Was it a childhood dream, or was it sparked by another interest?

"As a child, I was fascinated by aircraft and always felt a buzz of excitement when planes flew overhead. This is where my passion for flying initially began, but it wasn't until I carried out a career suitability test at college that I really started to consider cabin crew as a serious future prospect. The test examined personal attributes, interests and skills, and the final result came back suggesting suitability for the occupation. I done some further research into the job and instantly agreed. This job is tailored to my personality, skills and experience and is one I will feel committed to. Moreover, it is one I am confident that I will be good at."

Do you think the role of cabin crew is glamorous?

"Having thoroughly researched the position, I am aware that the glamour associated with the role is rather superficial. Sure there are benefits of travel, and the crew certainly do make themselves appear glamorous, but the constant travelling between time zones, the long and tiring shifts, unpredictable schedules and irregular working patterns place tough demands on crew and make the job anything but glamorous."

What do you think are the disadvantages of being cabin crew?

To deny the obvious drawbacks of the job will only make you sound naive and unprepared. So, be up front about the disadvantages and demonstrate that you have considered these carefully.

"The obvious disadvantages are the flight delays and cancellations that crew experience. While passengers also experience these issues, crew experience those far more often. This makes for very long and tiring shifts, irregular working patterns and unpredictable schedules.

Moreover, the regular crossing between different time zones can take its toll leading to jet lag and fatigue. Ultimately, though, these challenges are part of the job and, with some advance preparation, they can be managed to a certain degree."

What qualities do you think a good cabin crew member should have?

"Passengers generally spend more time with the cabin crew than with any other members of the airline staff, so they have a vital role in giving a good impression of the airline as a whole. This means crew members need to have good communication and customer care skills, as well as a friendly and welcoming demeanour.

Because of the importance of safety, it is also important that they have the strength of character to cope with difficult people and situations, in a calm and objective manner.

These are all attributes I possess, and are the primary reason I would complement your existing team."

Why should we hire you instead of someone with cabin crew experience?

"Although I might not have cabin crew experience, I have the necessary skills to make an impressive start, and the willingness to learn and improve. Sometimes, employers do better when they hire people who don't have a great deal of repetitive experience. That way, they can train these employees in their methods and ways of doing the job. Training is much easier than untraining."

Why should we hire you?

This is the time to shine, so don't be modest. Consider the experience and character traits that are most relevant and transferable to the position and, for greater impact, explain how you have demonstrated these in the past.

"As you can see from my résumé, I have worked in client facing roles for the past eight years. So, I am certainly qualified to perform the diverse requirements of this role. Also, the fact that I have been promoted through the ranks is a clear testament to my abilities and the confidence my manager had in me.

More significantly, my character is tailored to the role. As you will have observed during the group assessments, I am a very welcoming and social individual who interacts well with others. I readily adapt to new people and environments, I am hard working and think fast on my feet.

I am confident that these aspects of my personality and experience will enable me to perform the job to the same high standard that exists currently."

Why should we hire you for this position rather than another applicant?

"I can't tell you why you should hire me instead of another candidate but, I can tell you why you should hire me."

What do you know about our airline?

This is where your research will pay off handsomely. So, demonstrate your enthusiasm by sharing knowledge that will reveal the effort you have taken to learn more about the airline and its operations.

"Fly High Airlines began operating in 1980 with a single leased aircraft, serving just two destinations. The airline now serves 73 destinations in 48 countries worldwide and is rapidly expanding its route network, which is soon to include Bristol and Ohio.

As a testament to the airlines excellent standard of service, it has acquired over 250 international awards for customer service excellence, and is now one of the largest and popular airlines in the world."

Why do you want to work for us?

To make the greatest impact, begin with a personal story, but close with a demonstration of your knowledge and fit for the airline. This will make you stand out as an informed and enthusiastic individual who has something more to offer.

"My first passenger experience with Fly High Airlines was two years ago, on a flight from Dubai to Los Angeles. The service on board was so immaculate and welcoming, that I was instantly impressed. Following this experience I became a frequent flyer and, when I decided to apply for this position, I was in no doubt who I want to work for.

Once I started to research the airline further, I was pleased to discover that the airlines corporate culture holds true with my own values and beliefs. Specifically the open door policy and customer comfort initiatives. This discovery reinforced my desire further and confirmed my belief that I will indeed complement your existing team."

What do you dislike about your current job?

There will always be less than exciting aspects of a job, however, being critical about your job isn't going to create a positive impression. So, soften these aspects as much as possible and try to select minor examples, such as paperwork, lack of job security or opportunities for growth.

"I honestly can't think of any major dislikes. I don't think I'd be able to really excel if I weren't truly interested in the work, or if I were merely motivated by its financial rewards. I guess my answer will have to come under the category or nuisances.

The biggest nuisance is the paperwork. I realise the importance of documentation, and I cooperatively fill out the forms, but I'm always looking for efficiencies in that area that will get me out in front of the client where I belong."

Why did you leave your last job?

» No opportunities
"While I enjoyed working for my previous employer, and appreciate the skills I developed while I was there, I felt I was not being challenged enough in the job. After working my way up through the company, there were no further opportunities for advancement."

» Redundancy
"I survived the first layoffs, but unfortunately this one got me."

» Temporary position
"The job was only a temporary position which I took to broaden my experience."

Why were you fired?

If you were dismissed from any position, you need to be honest and say so. However, you should be tactful in your answer and turn it into a positive learning experience.

Never: Badmouth previous employers, colleagues or bosses, place blame, tell lies or reveal team incompatibility

» Incompatibility
"I was desperate for work and took the job without fully understanding the expectations. It turned out that my competencies were not a right match for the employer's needs so we agreed that it was time for me to move on to a position that would be more suitable. I certainly learnt a great deal from this experience, and it's not a mistake I will ever repeat."

» Personal reasons
"I had been going through a rough patch in my personal life which, unfortunately, upset my work life. It is regrettable and my circumstances have now changed, but I really wasn't in the position to avoid it at the time"

Why have you had so many jobs?

» Broaden experience
"I wanted to experience different jobs to broaden my knowledge, skills and experience. This has provided me with a very valuable and rounded skill set."

» Temporary positions
"Due to the lack of full time opportunities in my area, I was only able to secure short term contracts."

» Youth
In my youth, I was unsure about the direction I wanted to take in my career. I have matured a great deal since those days and am now interested in establishing myself into a long term opportunity.

Why were you unemployed for so long?

» Study
"I wanted to broaden my knowledge base, so I went back into full time study."

» Travel
"I wanted to experience the world before settling into a long term career. I am now well travelled and ready to commit."

» Youth
"In my youth, I felt confused about the direction I wanted my career to take. I am now much more mature and certain in my desired direction."

» Personal reasons
"Personal circumstances prohibited me from taking gainful employment, however, circumstances have now changed and I am ready to get back to work."

What is your greatest weakness?

The key to answering questions about weaknesses is to focus your response on those skills you are actively learning or planning to develop. This could be assertiveness or leadership. The point is, it is only a weakness because you haven't yet mastered it, and that is why you are working on developing those skills further. Importantly, you should avoid volunteering examples which involve key competencies, such as customer care or teamwork.

» Generic
"I recognise that my (...) skills are a potential area of improvement, which is why I am actively working on developing this area further through a part time (...) training course. Following completion of this course, I intend to further my abilities by studying (...)."

» Perfectionist
I tend to spend longer than necessary making sure that things are perfect, and sometimes get a little frustrated if I don't achieve excellence.

I did learn early on in my career that this slows output but, on the other hand, without such attention to detail the consistency and accuracy of my work could be affected. It is a difficult balancing act but I am working on finding a more balanced approach.

» Paperwork
"I realise the importance of paperwork, but I tend to procrastinate if I don't build it into my schedule. I'm always looking for efficiencies in that area that will get me out in front of the client where I belong."

Do you prefer to work alone or as part of a team?

"I am happy either way, and equally efficient at both. So, whether I prefer to work alone or in a team would depend on the best way to complete the job.

I do, however, have a preference towards team spirit. As well as the interaction, there is greater satisfaction when you share the joy of completing a task."

Have you stretched the truth today to gain a favourable outcome?

"Absolutely not. I haven't tried to be someone I am not, because I wouldn't want to get the job that way. To do so would be such a short term gain because eventually I would be found out."

How would you respond if we told you that you have been unsuccessful on this occasion?

"Naturally, I will be a disappointed if I do not secure this job with you because it is something I really want, I feel ready for it, and I have had plenty to contribute. However, I am not one to give up quickly. I will think about where I went wrong and how I could have done better, and I would then take steps towards strengthening my candidacy."

What would you say if I said your skills and experience were below the requirements of this job?

"I would ask what particular aspects of my skills and experience you felt were lacking and address each one of those areas with examples of where my skills and experiences do match your requirements. I would expect that after this discussion you would be left in no doubt about my ability to do this job."

I'm not sure you are suitable for the position. Convince me.

"I am absolutely suitable. In fact, I am confident that I am perfect for this position.

You are looking for someone who is customer focused. Well, as you can see from my résumé, I have worked in client facing roles for eight years so have had plenty of experience dealing with the various aspects. I also run a successful business that relies on customer satisfaction. The fact that I am still in business, and have a solid and increasing client base, is a clear testament to my abilities.

Furthermore, you need someone who has a calm approach, and retains their composure in the face of adversity. Again, I have demonstrated this capability on several occasions throughout my career.

Beyond this, I have a friendly and optimistic character. I am hard working, I thrive on challenges and will always strive to deliver the highest standard of service to your passengers.

I am confident that my skills, experience and personal qualities will complement your existing team and allow me to make a positive contribution to the airline's ongoing success."

How often do you lose your temper?

"I never lose my temper. I regard that sort of behaviour as counterproductive and inappropriate. By losing your temper, you cannot possibly resolve a problem. Even if you're completely right, losing your temper often destroys your ability to convince others of this."

Would you take this job if we offered it to you?

"Yes, definitely. I was eager as soon as I saw the job opening on your web site. More than that though, actually meeting potential colleagues and finding out more about the airline and the position has clarified still further what an exciting challenge it would be to work here."

Can we contact previous employers for references?

"Yes, absolutely. I'm confident that all my references will be favourable and will confirm what we've discussed here today."

23:00

Hypothetical Questions

" When you know what you want, and want it bad enough, you will find a way to get it"

- Jim Rohn

Hypothetical questions present candidates with difficult real-life situations, where almost any answer can be challenged.

A good way to approach these questions is to consider the feelings of everyone involved, and think about the implications for your colleagues and the airline.

Prove to the recruiters that you would be proactive and do your best to resolve the situation using your own initiative, whilst remembering that you could ask for the help of the more experienced crew if necessary.

If you have followed these guidelines and are still challenged, the recruiter may be testing your ability to manage conflict or stress. Bear in mind that if you are not cabin crew yet, you cannot really be expected to know the best reply so do not be tricked into entering into an argument with the recruiter.

In either case it is important to remain calm and focused, and to demonstrate that, although you appreciate there are many aspects to each situation, you would always be trying to find acceptable solutions.

If you really can't think of a solution, you can simply say, "That is a new area for me so I am afraid I can't really answer that, but I enjoy acquiring new knowledge and I do learn quickly."

How would you handle a passenger who is intoxicated?

"I would not provide any more alcoholic beverages. I would encourage food, and offer a cup of tea or coffee. If the situation worsens beyond my control, I would inform my senior and seek assistance from the other crew members."

What would you do if a commercially important passenger complained about a crying child?

"I would apologise to the passenger and offer my assistance to the guardian of the child."

How would you deal with a passenger who is scared of flying?

"Being aware of what to expect, and just realising that a plane's wings are supposed to flex and move around gently in flight, can help relieve anxiety. Similarly, the collection of bumps and bangs that always accompany a flight can be made less fearsome if they are expected. So, I would try to comfort the passenger by talking them through the flight, and reassuring them of any strange noises they may hear.

I would advise them where I can be found, and show them the call bell. I would then check on them periodically throughout the flight."

How would you deal with a passenger who is not, right but believes he is right?

"I would explain the company's rules and policies to the passenger in a calm, professional and positive manner. Hopefully, this should clarify any misconceptions that the passenger may have."

How would you handle a colleague who is being rude or racist?

"I would act immediately to put a stop to any racist or rude behaviour by making it clear to the person that their behaviour is not acceptable. If he or she continues, I would then report it to proper authority."

If you spotted a colleague doing something unethical or illegal, what would you do?

"I would act immediately to put a stop to any unethical or illegal activity. I would try to document the details of the incident and try to collect any physical evidence. Then I would report it to my senior."

What would you do if you suspect that a passenger is suspicious or a high risk to passengers?

"I would keep watch before reporting to the senior any abnormal behaviour indicating a suspicious passenger."

24:00

Interviewer Quesitons

> "To solve any problem, here are three questions to ask yourself: First, what could I do? Second, what could I read? And third, who could I ask?"
>
> **- Jim Rohn**

This section of the interview is a real chance for you to shine and set yourself apart from all the other candidates. Therefore, it is a good idea to prepare one or two intelligent questions in advance.

The questions you ask, and how you ask them, say a lot about you, your motives, your depth of knowledge about the airline and the position itself.

Guidelines

The questions you ask should follow these guidelines:

» Don't ask questions that could be easily answered through your own research.

» Ask questions which demonstrate a genuine interest in and knowledge of the airline and the position.

» Demonstrate that you know just that little bit more than is required.

Question About Suitability

Asking recruiters to raise their concerns about your suitability will provide you with an opportunity to follow up and reassure the recruiter.

» Do you have any reservations about my ability to do this job?

» What do you foresee as possible obstacles or problems I might have?

» Is there anything else I need to do to maximise my chances of getting this job?

» How does my background compare with others you have interviewed?

» Is there anything else you'd like to know?

» What do you think are my strongest assets and possible weaknesses?

» Do you have any concerns that I need to clear up in order to be a considered candidate?

Questions About the Recruiter

Asking recruiters about their views and experience in the job or working with the airline will demonstrate your genuine interest and motives.

» How did you find the transition in relocating to ...?

» Why did you choose to work at ... airlines?

» What is it about this airline that keeps you working here?

» It sounds as if you really enjoy working here, what have you enjoyed most about working for ... airlines?

General Questions

» How would you describe the company culture?

» I feel my background and experience are a good fit for this position, and I am very interested. What is the next step?

» Yes, when do I start?

No Questions

» I did have plenty of questions, but we've covered them all during our discussions. I was particularly interested in ... but we've dealt with that thoroughly.

» I had many questions, but you've answered them all you have been so helpful. I'm even more excited about this opportunity than when I applied.

Questions to Avoid

You should avoid asking questions such as those following as they will make you appear selfishly motivated.

» How many day's holiday allowances will I receive?

» What is the salary?

» When will I receive a pay increase?

» How many free flights will my family receive?

» Can I request flights to ...?